WITH

Fit to
Ski and
Snowb

Fit to ski and snowboard :

DATE DUE

OCT 0 2 2007	

DEMCO, INC. 38-2931

Snyde. R

Fit to Ski and Snowboard

The Skier's and Boarder's Guide to Strength and Conditioning

 Ragged Mountain Press / McGraw-Hill

Camden, Maine • New York • Chicago • San Francisco
New Delhi • San Juan • Seoul • Singapore • Sydney

ROCKY SNYDER, C.S.C.S.

Certified Strength and Conditioning Specialist

• Lisbon • London • Madrid • Mexico City • Milan •
• Toronto

1 2 3 4 5 6 7 8 9 DOC DOC 0 9 8 7 6

Library of Congress Cataloging-in-Publication Data
Snyder, Rocky.
  Fit to ski and snowboard : the skier's and boarder's guide to strength and conditioning / Rocky Snyder.
      p.   cm.
  Includes index.
  ISBN 0-07-146899-4 (pbk.)
  1. Skis and skiing—Training. 2. Snowboarding—Training. I. Title.
  GV854.85.S66 2006
  796.93—dc22   2006006587

Questions regarding the content of this book should be addressed to
    Ragged Mountain Press
    P.O. Box 220
    Camden, ME 04843
    www.raggedmountainpress.com

Questions regarding the ordering of this book should be addressed to
    The McGraw-Hill Companies
    Customer Service Department
    P.O. Box 547
    Blacklick, OH 43004
    Retail customers: 1-800-262-4729
    Bookstores: 1-800-722-4726

Title page photo by Image Source Limited/Index Stock Imagery.
Chapter opener photos: snowboarder courtesy Mount Sunapee; skier courtesy Image Source Limited/Index Stock Imagery.
Photos in Chapter 3 by Scott Lechner. All other photos by Gary Irving.
Illustration on page 218 by George Arentz.

To my wife Dana.
Thanks for keeping me warm
on those cold, snowy nights.

Contents

Acknowledgments

This book would not have been possible had it not been for the support of family, friends, and colleagues who continually encouraged me to follow through on an idea.

Special thanks to videographer/photographer Gary Irving for his patience and help through grueling hours of photographing all of the exercises. You are a great friend and workout partner.

Introduction

People of all ages are enjoying the slopes, and each year the numbers
keep rising. However, in today's world of time-saving and laborsaving
devices, many people have become less active on a day-to-day basis.
Many young skiers and snowboarders have video games, computers,
and DVD players that can keep them entertained for hours with mini-
mal activity. Most adults have office jobs and long commutes, which
reduce their activity level dramatically compared to their younger days.
This sedentary existence combined with infrequent bouts of activity
can lead to what has been called the weekend-warrior syndrome—
caused when a person experiences injury because he or she plays too
hard on the weekends, following a workweek that involves little physical activity.

Common injury sites for most snowboarders are the wrists, shoulders, and ankles, whereas most skiers' injuries involve the knees, hips,
and lower back. Younger snowboarders are more susceptible to elbow
fractures and dislocations, and those who perform high-speed maneuvers and jumps are more prone to head and neck injuries. All snowrid-
ers need a conditioning program that increases strength, endurance,
and flexibility while reducing the risk of injury. Articles in fitness and
skiing/snowboarding magazines sometimes feature an exercise or
stretch for winter enthusiasts, yet there is little information on complete conditioning programs. This book will not tell you how to carve
down mountains, where to find the best resorts, how to conquer the
half-pipe or the moguls, or how to master any of the basics. What it will
do is provide the tools you need to be better conditioned for the activity you so enjoy.

Sport-specific training is an area in which many health clubs fall
short. When someone joins a commercial gym, this new member usually determines an exercise program with the help of a staff member.
The typical program is a general conditioning routine designed for
overall fitness—not for a particular sport. The program resembles more
of a bodybuilder's workout, concentrating on a couple of muscle

groups one day and others the next. Unless medical concerns require adjustments, most exercise programs will be very similar. Although not necessarily bad, these generic programs could be better designed to meet the specific goals of the individual. Snowboarding and skiing require the entire body to work synergistically, and the workouts should be more specific to reflect this need.

Fit to Ski and Snowboard offers a comprehensive, sport-specific approach to conditioning. It is designed to fight the weekend-warrior syndrome safely and effectively. The programs described here can be adapted for use by anyone, regardless of gender, age, or fitness level. You do not have to be a member of a health club to use this approach effectively. Many of the exercises can be performed at home.

The chapters of this book detail how to create a personalized conditioning routine; describe exercises that contribute to strength, endurance, and flexibility; and give sample conditioning programs for both gym and home.

Before you start, here are a few basic rules to follow:

- Before beginning any new exercise program, it is strongly recommended that you consult your primary health-care provider.

- Execute proper form during all exercises and stretches. If the form is incorrect, different muscles must compensate—and the more compensation that occurs, the higher the potential for injury.

- If you experience dizziness, discomfort, or pain, stop immediately.

- The final rule: Have fun!

For more information or to contact me at Devotion2*Motion* Consultants, go to www.devotion2motion.net.

heart rate. Multiply that maximum heart rate by the desired exercise percentage (intensity) that you select (most likely between 65 and 85 percent) to find your target heart rate. For example, the theoretical maximum heart rate for a 40-year-old snowboarder would be 180; multiplying by a desired percentage of, for example, 70 percent would result in a target exercise heart rate of 126. This is the simplest way to determine a target heart rate.

A better equation—the Karvonen Method—uses both a person's resting heart rate and age to determine the target heart rate. The best time to take your resting heart rate is in the morning, before getting out of bed. Count your pulse for 1 minute. This is your resting heart rate. The equation is as follows:

Maximum Heart Rate (220 – Age) – Resting Heart Rate x Desired Percent + Resting Heart Rate = Target Exercise Heart Rate

For example, a 50-year-old woman with a resting heart rate of 63 beats per minute wishes to exercise at an intensity of 75 percent of her maximum heart rate. Her target heart rate would be determined as follows:

220 – 50 (age) = 170 (maximum heart rate)
170 – 63 (resting heart rate) = 107
107 x 0.75 (desired percent) = 80
80 + 63 (resting heart rate) = 143 (target heart rate)

Using a measurement known as the rate of perceived exertion (RPE) is a more subjective way to determine your desired intensity level. Simply put, on a scale from 1 to 10 (1 being very easy and 10 being maximal effort), how intensely do you think you are exercising? To determine your own personal target zone, warm up and then build to a submaximal yet challenging effort after a few minutes of an endurance activity, such as running or jumping rope. Your heart rate at that point will be your target heart rate and will be between 5 and 8 on your RPE scale. Ideally, a person should exercise between 5 and 8 on that scale with short bursts of work in the 9 to 10 range. Using both the Karvonen Method and the rate of perceived exertion can provide a more accurate estimate of the correct intensity level for your endurance training.

Strength, Balance, and Core Training

Strength training consists of relatively short bursts of muscular force that last between 1 second and 2 minutes. This type of training helps build size and strength in the muscles and conditions them to store more energy for immediate use. One or two days per week of strength training is considered a maintenance routine that produces little change in strength levels. Three or more days of strength training brings about physiological changes. Strength training sessions may range from 10 minutes to 2 hours or more depending on the training protocol. I generally recommend 30 minutes to 1 hour, three to five days per week, to begin to experience the physiological benefits of this kind of training.

Balance training is performed on unstable surfaces, such as stability balls, wobble boards, balance boards, and foam rolls. The benefits of this approach include enhancing strength and coordination in the smaller stabilizing muscles of the body, enhancing kinesthetic awareness (the mind's awareness of where the body is in space), and improving the body's sense of balance. Be sure to master executing the traditional strength training exercises with proper form and control before advancing to performing the same exercises on the balance apparatus.

Core training involves strength exercises that focus on the muscles of the trunk (the abdominals, obliques, lower back muscles, and so forth). Most exercises will incorporate flexing, extending, rotating, or side bending the spine, or a combination of movements performed in conjunction with upper and lower body motion. The purpose of core training is to strengthen the muscles that protect the back while at the same time allowing force to transfer from the center of the body down through the legs and up through the arms with the least amount of restriction. For example, in order to carve powerful turns on the slopes, the arms and shoulders must work with the legs to initiate and complete a turn; if the muscles that surround the trunk are weak, the turn will be weak because upper and lower body forces are not well connected.

- When performing strength, balance, and core training exercises, start by executing 1 or 2 sets of each exercise selected.

- After exercising for a week, increase the sets from 2 to 4 per session.

- With most exercises, perform between 8 and 15 repetitions in a set.

- If you cannot do an exercise with proper form for 8 repetitions, chances are the weight is too heavy.

- If you can do an exercise with proper form for more than 15 repetitions, the weight is probably too light.

- For exercises that do not incorporate the external resistance of weights (such as dumbbells or barbells), you can magnify the intensity by increasing the repetitions. Among these non-weighted exercises are abdominal and lower back exercises, push-ups, and pull-ups. Each set can include 10 to 30 repetitions.

It's a good idea to change your list of exercises on a regular basis so that your muscles don't get too accustomed to the same movement. The more variety you add to a strength workout, the greater the variety of demands you place upon the muscles—with the advantage that it forces them to adapt in multiple ways. Try changing the list of exercises each week or every other week. It's OK to repeat some of the same exercises, but be sure to alternate at least two or three of them.

Plyometric Training

Plyometrics are exercises primarily consisting of hops, leaps, jumps, and bounds. The repetition of these actions brings about some of the most powerful muscular reactions the body can manifest. The basic theory behind plyometrics can best be explained by what happens during a physical examination at the doctor's office. The doctor takes a little rubber hammer and taps your leg just below the knee cap when you are sitting on the examination table. The knee-jerk reaction causes your leg to kick forward. What has occurred is a rapid stretching of the tendon and muscle, one so fast that the body's natural response is for the muscle to contract (shorten) to prevent injury to the connective tissue. This contraction becomes even more powerful when more force is applied.

Each time a person hops, jumps, leaps, or bounds, the return to the ground creates that same stretch-shortening reflex. The ensuing reaction is a powerful muscular contraction. The more this response is trained, the greater the power potential that exists. One measurement of such power is the vertical jump test. It is easy to perform and can be a fun way of seeing marked improvement. Standing beside a wall, rub some chalk on your middle finger. With your feet flat, reach as high as possible and make a mark on the wall. Rub more chalk on your middle finger, and then jump and touch the wall as high as you can. Measure the distance between both marks. This is roughly your vertical jump. Standards for this test vary from one association to the next, but a measurement of 15 to 20 inches generally is considered above average. Measurements greater than 20 inches are considered excellent.

Because of the intense ballistic nature of these exercises, they are not recommended for those new to training and conditioning. Following are two ways to gauge whether you're ready for plyometric training:

- Successfully perform 5 repetitions of the squat using 50 percent of your body weight on a barbell (see pages 116–20).

- Successfully perform 5 repetitions of the single-leg squat (see pages 127–28).

During plyometric training, each time you return to the ground is called a contact (repetition). Beginners should start with 2 sets of 5 to 10 contacts for each chosen exercise and not let the total number of contacts exceed 60. Intermediate-level workouts should include 2 to 3 sets of 8 to 12 contacts (not to exceed 100 contacts). For advanced workouts, perform 3 to 4 sets of 8 to 12 contacts and do not exceed 150.

Workout Programs

Chapter 7 provides detailed sample workout programs, including exercises for flexibility, endurance, and strength. One program is a ten-week plan for use at a gym or health club; the other is a ten-week program that encompasses the same conditioning goals but can be carried out at home.

Chapter 2

Flexibility Training

One of the most important—yet most often overlooked—elements in fitness is flexibility. When muscles have more tension than they should, an imbalance is created and the body's movement is restricted. This makes any activity require more effort.

It is through lengthening (stretching) tense muscles and tightening (strengthening) weak muscles that the body is restored to a balanced state. The more balanced the body, the more efficient its movements—and the less likely an injury is to occur. The following pages contain photos and descriptions of stretching exercises that help create a better balance of tension and thus contribute to flexibility.

Stretching exercises are often referred to as poses because the stretch puts the body into a pose that will be held for a period of time. Holding a pose for 10 seconds is good, but maintaining it for 30 seconds to 1 minute allows more time for muscles to balance. Performing the stretch more than once can also bring better results.

If any stretch causes pain, stop immediately and omit it from your program for the time being. As your body achieves greater balance, you will be able to reincorporate certain stretches that previously caused pain. Every body is different. Therefore, not all poses are effective for everyone.

The following stretches or poses are grouped into four categories: lying, kneeling, sitting, and standing. When creating your own flexibility program, choose a few stretches from each category in order to benefit a full range of muscles.

The photos and descriptions in this chapter are designed to familiarize you with the stretches and to serve as a reference once you've started your training routine. Chapter 7 provides detailed workout programs that incorporate these various stretches.

Lying Stretches

Crossed Knee Lift

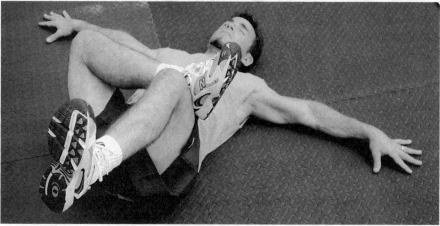

1. Lie on the floor faceup, with arms straight out from the sides of your body and palms down.

2. Cross one ankle over the opposite knee.

3. Lift the knee up directly above the hip and hold for 15 seconds to 1 minute.

4. Repeat using the opposite leg.

Benefit: Promotes proper muscular balance in the hips and back.

Crossover Twist

1. Lie on the floor faceup, with arms straight out from the sides of your body and palms down.

2. Bend the knees at right angles so your feet are flat on the floor.

3. Cross one ankle over the opposite knee.

4. Keeping shoulders and arms on the floor, rotate the leg and the crossed foot over to the side until both rest on the floor.

5. The knee that is not on the floor should point up to the ceiling.

6. Hold for 10 seconds to 1 minute.

7. Repeat using the opposite leg and foot.

Benefit: Promotes proper muscular balance of the hips and lower back.

Upper Spinal Floor Twist

1. Lie on one side, with your knees pulled up into right angles with your hips and ankles.

2. Extend your arms in front of your body, with palms together. [1]

3. Exhale as you reach over your body with the upper arm and down to the floor on the opposite side. [2]

4. Keep your legs firmly anchored to the floor so the rotation occurs in the spine and torso.

5. Hold for 10 seconds to 1 minute.

6. Repeat on the opposite side.

Benefit:
Promotes proper spinal rotation and torso flexibility.

lying stretches

Straight-Leg Hamstring Stretch with Strap

lying stretches

1. Lie on the floor faceup, with a strap wrapped around the arch of one foot.

2. Hold one end of the strap in each hand.

3. Lift the straight leg up in the direction of the shoulder.

4. When you feel a stretch in the hamstring, apply gentle tension to the strap by pulling with your arms.

5. Hold each stretch for at least 2 seconds.

6. Perform 5 to 10 sets before changing legs.

7. Repeat using a bent knee.

Benefit: Reduces knee, hip, and lower back tension.

Calf Stretch with Strap

1. Lie on the floor faceup, with a strap wrapped around the ball of one foot.

2. Hold one end of the strap in each hand.

3. Begin the stretch with the straight leg above the hip.

4. Point the foot upward, and then flex the foot downward toward your head.

5. When you feel a stretch in the calf, apply gentle tension to the strap by pulling with your arms.

6. Hold each stretch for at least 2 seconds.

7. Perform 5 to 10 repetitions before changing legs.

Benefit: Reduces ankle and knee tension.

Intense Front Stretch

1. Sit on the floor with your hands flat behind the hips, knees slightly bent, feet flat and hip-width apart. [1]

2. Exhale and lift your hips off the floor, tilt your head backward, and straighten your legs and arms. [2]

3. Hold for 10 seconds to 1 minute.

Benefit: Reduces ankle tension, stretches the chest, and strengthens arms and hips.

Locust Pose

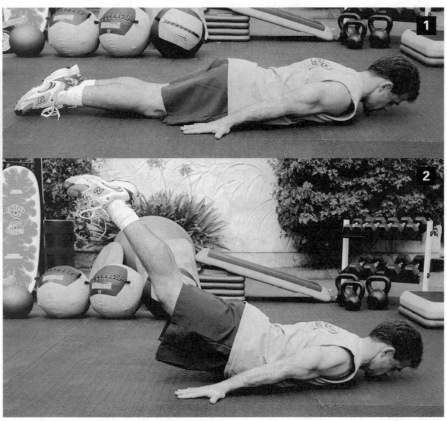

1. Lie facedown with your legs straight and your hands palms down just outside the thighs. [1]

2. Exhale and lift your legs as you press your palms into the floor. [2]

3. Hold for 2 to 10 seconds.

4. Perform 5 to 10 repetitions.

Benefit: Strengthens lower back muscles.
Note: People with lower back problems should avoid this exercise.

Bridge Pose

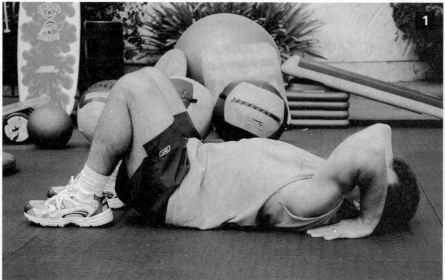

1. Lie on your back with knees bent, feet flat, and hands palms down beside your head. [1]

continued

Bridge Pose, *continued*

2. Exhale and press your feet and hands into the floor while lifting your hips and shoulders. [2]

3. Hold for 10 seconds to 1 minute.

4. Perform 5 to 10 repetitions.

Benefit: Strengthens shoulders, thighs, and lower back muscles.

Bow Pose

1. Lie facedown with your knees bent and your heels close to the buttocks.

2. Clasp your ankles with your hands.

3. Exhale as you lift your torso and legs off the floor.

4. Hold for 2 to 10 seconds.

5. Perform 5 to 10 repetitions.

Benefit: Stretches chest, abdominals, and hip flexor muscles and promotes better spine mobility.

Upward Dog

1. Begin in a push-up position, with arms and legs supporting your straight body above the floor.

2. Inhale as you bend your arms and lower your body toward the floor—but do not touch the floor.

3. Exhale as you pull your chest forward and upward and press your arms into a straightened position.

4. Perform at least 2 sets of 2 to 10 repetitions.

Benefit: Promotes spinal flexibility and upper body strength.

Kneeling Stretches

Hero Pose

1. Kneel with your feet slightly wider than hip-width apart.

2. Lower the hips back and to the floor between both heels while maintaining a tall, upright posture.

3. Hold for 10 seconds to 1 minute.

Benefit: Stretches thigh muscles and promotes knee mobility.

kneeling stretches

Reclining Hero Pose

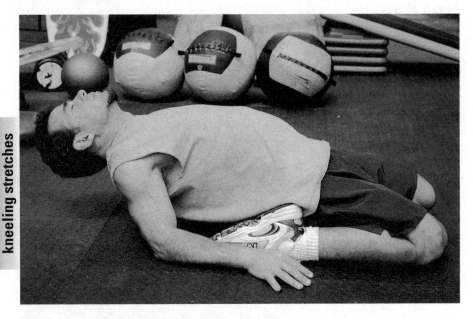

1. Kneel with your feet slightly wider than hip-width apart.

2. Lower the hips back and to the floor between both heels while supporting the upper body with both elbows.

3. Hold for 10 seconds to 1 minute.

Benefit: Stretches thigh and hip flexor muscles and promotes knee and spine mobility.

Kneeling Groin Stretch

1. Kneel on one knee with the opposite foot forward (both knees should be at right angles).

2. Exhale as you shift your body forward while maintaining a tall, upright posture.

3. Hold for 10 seconds to 1 minute.

4. Repeat using the opposite leg.

Benefit: Stretches thigh, hip flexor, and groin muscles.

Kneeling Single Quadriceps Stretch

1. Place your right knee on the floor with the top of your right foot on a bench.

2. Place your left foot on the floor in front of your body so the left knee is at a right angle.

3. Raise your upper body above your hips in a tall posture.

4. Hold for 10 seconds to 1 minute.

5. Repeat using the opposite leg.

Benefit: Stretches the quadriceps and hip flexor muscles and enhances balance.

Child's Pose

1. Kneel with both hips resting on your heels.

2. Exhale as you lean forward until your chest rests on your thighs and your head rests on the floor.

3. Place your arms by your sides with your palms facing up.

4. Hold for 10 seconds to 1 minute.

Benefit: Stretches lower back muscles and promotes hip, knee, and ankle mobility.

Mad Cat Stretch

1. Support your body on all fours, with your hands below the shoulders and your knees below the hips. [1]

2. Breathe out as you arch your back upward. [2]

3. Breathe in as you bow your back downward.

4. Move your head in the opposite direction of the back.

5. The movement should be continuous, without pausing at the top or the bottom.

Benefit: Promotes better movement in the back, shoulders, and hips.

Downward Dog

kneeling stretches

1. Support your body on all fours, with your hands below the shoulders and your knees below the hips.

2. Exhale as you push your body backward onto your hands and feet while straightening the legs, arms, and back.

3. Press your heels to the floor, keeping the legs straight, and push your hips away from your hands.

4. Point the sit bones at the base of the buttocks upward.

5. Hold for 10 seconds to 1 minute.

Benefit: Stretches the calves and hamstrings, reduces tension in the lower back, and increases shoulder strength.

Arm Circles

1. Extend your arms out from the sides of your body at shoulder height.

2. Keep your shoulder blades pinched together as you make 6-inch arm circles backward with your palms faceup.

3. Flip your palms down and reverse the circle direction.

4. Keep the body as still as possible, with movement occurring only at the shoulder joint.

Benefit: Promotes ball-and-socket movement in the shoulders.
Note: This exercise can be performed kneeling, seated, or standing.

kneeling stretches

Shoulder Pivots

1. Place the knuckles of your index and middle fingers against the temples of your head.

2. Face your palms forward, with the thumbs below the fingers. [1]

3. Exhale as you pull your elbows forward until they touch. [2]

4. Inhale as you pull your elbows back as far as possible.

5. The knuckles should act like hinges on a door; do not lift them off the temples.

6. Perform 1 to 3 sets of 10 to 30 repetitions.

Benefit: Promotes proper shoulder joint movement and strengthens the rotator cuff muscles.

Note: This exercise can be performed kneeling, seated, or standing.

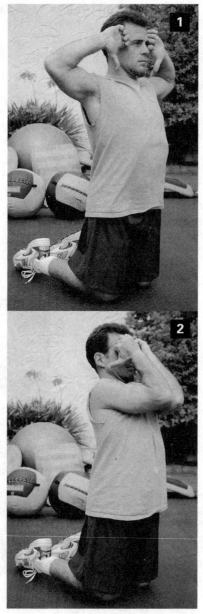

kneeling stretches

Sitting Stretches

Fingers and Toes Entwined

1. Sit with your legs straight in front of your body.

2. Cross your left ankle over your right knee.

3. Interlock the fingers of your right hand with the toes of your left foot.

4. Rotate your left foot clockwise, then counterclockwise.

5. Flex and point your right foot.

6. Perform each movement 10 to 15 times before changing motions.

7. Repeat using the left hand and right foot.

Benefit: Promotes proper ankle movement.

sitting stretches

Archer Pose

1. Sit with your legs straight in front of your body.

2. Bend your right leg and grip the arch of your right foot with both hands. [1]

sitting stretches

3. Gently straighten your right leg while maintaining a tall, upright posture. [2]

4. Hold for 10 seconds to 1 minute.

5. Repeat using the opposite leg.

Benefit: Stretches the arms, hamstrings, and calf muscles.

Sitting Floor

1. Sit tall with both legs straight in front of your body, with your feet pointing up.

2. Wrap a strap around the balls of both feet and grip one end in each hand.

3. Apply tension to the strap and pull the feet toward you while maintaining a tall, upright posture.

4. Hold for 10 seconds to 1 minute.

Benefit: Promotes hip and back strength while stretching the hamstrings and calf muscles.

Simple Twist

1. In a seated position, bring your right leg behind your body by bending the right knee.

2. Place the sole of your left foot against the top of your right knee and thigh.

3. Remain in a tall, seated position as you reach back behind your body with your left hand and twist your torso to the left.

4. Keep your left hand anchored to the floor and bring your right hand to the left knee to help you twist.

5. Hold for 10 seconds to 1 minute before switching sides.

Benefit: Improves flexibility of the spine, waist, and front side of the hip.

Seated Torso Twist

1. Sit in a chair, with your knees parallel and at right angles to the hips and ankles. Your feet should point straight ahead.

2. Remain in a tall, seated posture as you twist your torso to the right and you reach around to the top of the backrest with your right hand.

3. Hold on to your right knee or the bottom-right corner of the seat with the left hand.

4. Keep your hips and legs facing forward so the rotation occurs in the spine and torso.

5. Hold for 10 seconds to 1 minute before switching sides.

Benefit: Improves torso and lower back flexibility.

Wrist Stretch 1

1. Extend your left arm in front of you with the palm facing up.

2. Place your right hand, palm down, on your left fingers.

3. Wrap your right thumb around the back of your left hand.

4. Gently pull your left fingers down with your right hand, using your right thumb as a brace, so your left wrist extends.

5. Hold for 10 seconds to 1 minute.

6. Repeat using the opposite hand.

Benefit: Stretches the wrist and forearm muscles.

Note: This exercise can be performed seated or standing.

Wrist Stretch 2

sitting stretches

1. Extend your left arm in front of you with the palm facing down.

2. Place your right hand, palm down, on your left knuckles.

3. Wrap your right thumb around the front of your left hand.

4. Gently pull your left hand down with your right hand, using your right thumb as a brace, so your left wrist flexes.

5. Hold for 10 seconds to 1 minute.

6. Repeat using the opposite hand.

Benefit: Stretches the wrist and forearm muscles.

Note: This exercise can be performed seated or standing.

-

-

Evanston Public Library
Phone renewal 847-590-8706
Sign up for email notices.
Visit www.epl.org

Date due: 12/20/2016,23:59
Title: Fit to ski and snowboard : the skie
r's and boarde
Author: Snyder, Rocky.
Item ID: 31192013387731
Call number: 796.93 Snyde.R
Current time: 11/22/2016,10:23

Date due: 12/20/2016,23:59
Title: Ultimate skiing
Author: LeMaster, Ron, 1949-
Item ID: 31192014501017
Call number: 796.93 Lemas.R
Current time: 11/22/2016,10:23

Wrist Twist

1. With your arms bent at the elbows, grip your left hand, palm facing away, with your right hand, palm facing you.

2. With your right hand, twist your left hand and wrist toward you.

3. Hold for 10 seconds to 1 minute.

4. Repeat reversing the position of the hands.

Benefit: Enhances wrist rotation and stretches the forearm muscles.

Note: This exercise can be performed seated or standing.

sitting stretches

Standing Stretches

Triangle Pose

1. Stand with your legs 3 feet apart.

2. Keep the right foot pointing forward and turn the left foot sideways so the feet are perpendicular to each other.

3. Extend your arms out from the sides of your body at shoulder height. [1]

4. Bend your hip and waist to the left so the left hand contacts the lower portion of the left leg.

5. Turn your head upward. [2]

6. Hold for 10 seconds to 1 minute before switching sides.

Benefit: Stretches and strengthens muscles at the hips and waist.

Reverse Triangle Pose

1. Stand with your legs 3 feet apart.

2. Keep the right foot pointing forward and turn the left foot sideways so the feet are perpendicular to each other.

3. Extend your arms out from the sides of your body at shoulder height. [1]

4. Bend and rotate your hip and waist to the left so your right hand contacts the lower portion of the left leg.

5. Turn your head upward. [2]

6. Hold for 10 seconds to 1 minute before switching sides.

Benefit: Stretches and strengthens muscles at the hips, waist, and lower back.

Warrior Pose

1. Stand with your legs 3 feet apart.

2. Keep your right foot pointing forward and turn your left foot sideways so your feet are perpendicular to each other.

3. Extend your arms out from the sides of your body at shoulder height. [1]

4. Bend your left knee while your right leg remains straight as you shift your body's weight sideways to the left. Turn your head to the left. [2]

5. Hold for 10 seconds to 1 minute before switching sides.

Benefit: Stretches the inner thigh and strengthens leg and core muscles.

Side Reach

1. Stand with your legs 3 feet apart.

2. Keep your right foot pointing forward and turn your left foot sideways so your feet are perpendicular to each other.

3. Extend your arms out from the sides of your body at shoulder height.

4. Bend your left knee, keeping your right leg straight, as you shift your body's weight sideways to the left.

5. Lower your left hand to contact the left ankle as you reach up and over your head with your right arm.

6. Hold for 10 seconds to 1 minute before switching sides.

Benefit: Stretches the torso muscles while strengthening the leg muscles.

Extended Toe-to-Hand Pose

1. Standing on your left leg, raise your right knee and grip the toes of your right foot with your right hand. [1]

2. Straighten your right leg and arm in front of you while maintaining a tall, upright posture. [2]

3. Hold for 10 seconds to 1 minute.

4. Repeat using the opposite hand and foot.

Benefit: Enhances balance and stretches the arms, hamstrings, and calf muscles.

Note: If you are unable to grip your foot with your hand and maintain proper form, place your heel on an object the same height as your hips and keep your arms hanging by your sides. For more intensity, grip the extended foot with both hands.

Squat Pose 1

1. Stand with your feet together and your arms extended in front of you. [1]

2. Bend at your knees and lower your body until your buttocks rest against your heels.

3. Balance on your toes while maintaining a tall, upright posture. [2]

4. Hold for 10 seconds to 1 minute.

Benefit: Promotes balance and enhances knee and ankle mobility.

standing stretches

Squat Pose 2

1. Stand with your feet together and your arms extended in front of you. [1]

2. Bend at your knees and lower your body until your buttocks rest against your heels.

3. Balance with your feet flat while maintaining a tall, upright posture. [2]

4. Hold for 10 seconds to 1 minute.

Benefit: Promotes balance, stretches lower back muscles, and enhances knee and ankle mobility.

Doorknob Stretch

1. Hold on to both knobs of an open door while standing straight. [1]
2. Pull your hips behind you and bend forward. [2]
3. Hold for 10 seconds to 1 minute.

Benefit: Stretches the lower back and hamstrings.

Dancer's Pose

standing stretches

1. Bend your right knee and grip the front of your right ankle with your right hand while extending your left arm in front of you.

2. Pull your right heel toward your right buttock.

3. Bend at the hips and lower your upper body until it is parallel with the floor. Your left arm should be in alignment with your upper body and your left leg should be slightly bent.

4. Hold for 10 seconds to 1 minute.

5. Repeat using the opposite arm and leg.

Benefit: Stretches the quadriceps and hip flexor muscles and enhances single-leg balance.

Standing Forward Bend

1. Stand tall with your feet hip-width apart and your arms extended in front of you. [1]

2. Exhale as you lower your upper body and reach your hands to the floor. [2]

3. Maintain a muscular contraction in your thighs to keep your legs straight.

4. Hold for 10 seconds to 1 minute.

5. Inhale as you return your upper body to the starting posture.

Benefit: Stretches the lower back and hamstrings.

Note: Two variations to this pose are as follows:

    a. Place your feet 4 to 5 feet apart and bend forward.

    b. Cross one leg in front of the other and perform the forward bend. Be sure to repeat with the opposite leg in front.

standing stretches

Arm Stretch

standing stretches

1. Stand with your arms extended in front of you, hands together and fingers laced.

2. Rotate your arms so your palms face forward. [1]

3. Raise your straight arms over your head and reach gently upward. [2]

4. Hold for 10 seconds to 1 minute.

Benefit: Stretches the wrists, arms, shoulders, chest, and outer back muscles.

Wrist Stretch

1. Stand 12 inches away from a wall.

2. Bend your elbows at right angles and place your palms against the wall with your fingers pointing to the floor.

3. Hold for 10 seconds to 1 minute.

Benefit: Improves wrist and forearm flexibility.

standing stretches

Chapter 3

Sun Salutation

The Sun Salutation is a series of gentle, flowing yoga poses that are often performed as a morning wake-up routine or as a warm-up routine prior to strength training. The Sun Salutation can also be performed as a warm-up routine before hitting the slopes. This series of movements enhances flexibility of the spine, legs, and chest while strengthening the arms and shoulders and enhancing the body's sense of balance and coordination.

Try to hold each pose for 5 to 15 seconds before transitioning to the next pose in the sequence. Perform the series of 12 poses three or four times. When performing the repetition of the lunge position, be sure to alternate legs. A single sequence of the 12 poses usually takes about 1 minute.

Concentrate to maintain an awareness of your breath while entering and exiting each pose. When breathing, be sure to inhale into the diaphragm, filling the midsection as deeply as possible.

Prayer Pose

1. Stand tall with your feet hip-width apart.

2. Gently press your palms together in a prayer position.

3. Inhale deeply.

Mountain Pose

1. Exhale as you reach upward with both arms.

Forward Bend

sun salutation

1. Inhale as you bend your body forward.
2. Lower your torso, with your arms reaching forward.
3. Bring your hands to the floor as you bend your back slightly.

Lunge Position

1. Bend both knees, with your hands flat on the floor.

2. Exhale as you step back with your right foot until the left knee is at a right angle.

3. Allow your midsection to rest against the top of your left thigh.

Plank Position

1. Bring your left leg back parallel to the right leg.

2. Inhale as you keep your arms straight to support the body's weight.

3. Keep your torso and legs straight so the body resembles a plank.

Grasshopper Pose

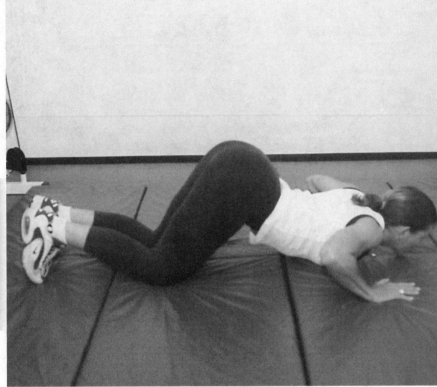

1. From the plank position, bend at the elbows and knees.

2. Exhale as you allow your body to lower until your chest almost scrapes the floor.

Upward-Facing Dog

1. Inhale as you press your chest upward and forward as your arms and legs straighten.

2. Keep the thigh muscles contracted to help support your body.

Downward-Facing Dog

1. Exhale as you push your body backward onto your hands and feet as the legs, arms, and back straighten.

2. Press your heels to the floor, while maintaining straight legs, and push the hips away from the hands.

3. Point the sit bones at the base of the buttocks upward.

Lunge Position

1. Bend both knees, with your hands flat on the floor.

2. Inhale as you step forward with the right foot until the right knee is at a right angle.

3. Allow your midsection to rest against the top of your right thigh.

Deep Forward Bend

1. Bring your left foot forward to be parallel with the right foot.

2. Exhale as you bend your body forward.

3. Inhale as you raise your torso, with your arms parallel with the spine.

Mountain Pose

1. Exhale as you reach upward with both arms.

Prayer Pose

1. Stand tall with your feet together as you lower your arms.

2. Gently press your palms together in a prayer position.

3. Inhale deeply.

4. Repeat the entire sequence of poses.

Chapter 4

Endurance Training

A snowrider requires not only flexibility and strength for cranking powerful turns but also muscular endurance to maintain stamina for all-day sessions. In creating an effective endurance program of cardiovascular activities, four elements are critical:

- **Frequency:** The number of times the endurance exercise is performed in a particular period of time.

- **Duration:** The length of time it takes to perform the exercise.

- **Intensity:** The effort level reached during the exercise.

- **Type:** The choice of exercise performed in a workout.

Increasing or upgrading any of these elements will increase the demands placed on your body as it works to develop the cardiovascular fitness essential to endurance.

This chapter concentrates on cardiovascular exercises that either are specific to snowriding (such as skateboarding, using the slideboard, surfing, and performing gymnastic maneuvers on a trampoline) or can serve as cross-training activities (such as running, cycling, rope jumping, and snowshoeing).

It's helpful at this point to understand the *overload principle*—the general idea that overloading or exhausting muscles carefully and systematically can produce physiological changes that make the muscles stronger and more durable. For example, a person snowboarding for the first time quickly becomes exhausted—not to mention badly bruised. But with a program of progressively tougher workouts, that individual should grow stronger as his or her muscles are taxed to a higher and higher point of fatigue. This principle will come into play as you develop a program of increasingly rigorous endurance activities.

The photos and descriptions that follow will familiarize you with various endurance drills and exercises. You can refer back to them as you progress in your personal training program. See Chapter 7 for detailed programs that include these exercises and offer recommendations on duration and intensity of the workouts.

Skateboarding

Skateboarding is one of the best ways to snowboard when there is no snow. Skateboarding and snowboarding are almost identical in their movements; it's just that the asphalt tends to hurt a little more than snow when you wipe out. Be sure to wear protective equipment (helmet, wrist guards, elbow pads) even if your friends point and laugh. The last thing you need is a road rash just before the first snowfall. Skate parks—which are becoming more common across the country—provide the perfect traffic-free environment to keep your board skills honed. Also, a long downhill stretch of road without cross streets could be the perfect place to practice carving. Avoid high-traffic areas! Cars tend to win head-on collisions.

Surfing

Obviously, if you don't live where there are waves, you are out of luck. But if you live near the coast and haven't yet tried surfing, consider taking a few lessons. The movement is similar to snowboarding, but how you distribute your weight is different. As on the slopes, surfing has rules of etiquette that need to be honored for your safety as well as others'. Also, certain surf spots considered "black diamonds" should not be surfed by beginners. Go to your local surf shop and ask the staff about the best places to learn.

Slide-Board

Using a slide-board is great conditioning for skiing, skating, and snowboarding. Whereas most other endurance exercises move in a forward and backward linear pattern and involve very little lateral (sideways) movement, using a slide-board works the muscles responsible for lateral movement—the same muscles that keep the body stable and balanced for snowboarding. Slide-boards with adjustable stoppers at the ends are recommended because they allow you to increase the distance as you become more familiar with the movement.

Start by placing the cloth slippers or booties that come with the board on your shoes. This allows you to slide with the least amount of friction. To help avoid falling, when approaching the slide-board place one foot on the stopper before placing the other foot on the slide. Brace the outer edge of the foot that is on the stopper against the stopper's edge, giving the foot a place to push off from. As the foot pushes off the stopper, the other foot, which is on the slide, will kick out sideways toward the opposite stopper. The arms will also swing in that direction, sending the body across the slide-board and landing on the opposite stopper. Be sure to brace the foot against the stopper when repeating the movement to return to the starting side. Continue this side-to-side motion for the designated amount of time. Stop if your pulse exceeds your target heart rate, and continue only after it returns to the target zone. For lower body intensity, clasp your hands behind your back while sliding.

Trampoline Work

If you are looking to step up your skill level with some aerials or a half-pipe routine, using a trampoline is essential. For safety and proper instruction, visit your local gymnastics center and take a class. After you have mastered the basics of jumping, add a bounce board to your workout. Similar in size and shape to a snowboard, a bounce board is designed to be worn while practicing on a trampoline. Proceed with extreme caution.

Walking and Running

Whether you walk or run doesn't really matter; either way, you'll reach the same destination eventually. Both are good choices as part of an endurance training routine.

Whichever you choose, stand as tall as possible. Keep your head over your shoulders, with your chest up and your hips tucked under. Let your arms swing freely forward and backward, and keep your feet pointing straight ahead. Start with 20 minutes and build from there. (Refer to the sample programs in Chapter 7 for additional recommended times.)

Stair Climbing

Cross-training with stair-climbing machines at a health club can provide a good workout. But if there is a long flight of stairs in your neighborhood—preferably made of wood rather than unforgiving concrete—try going up and down those for an endurance workout.

When climbing stairs, maintain the same form as when running or walking: stand tall, with your chest up and your hips tucked under. Walk slowly on the way down to allow your body and heart rate to recover. We will return to the stairs in Chapter 6, Plyometric Training, for other exercises of a more explosive nature. (Refer to the sample programs in Chapter 7 for recommended times.)

Jumping Rope

Jumping rope is a great overall conditioning exercise that promotes endurance in the upper and lower body and the trunk. Many varieties of jump ropes are available: cotton, nylon, rawhide, solid rubber, and ones with heavy handles. I prefer solid rubber jump ropes because the centrifugal force of the heavier rubber makes the wrists, forearms, and upper arms work harder the faster you jump—a definite plus for skiing and snowboarding. Be sure to choose a proper jumping surface—such as grass, sand, or a wooden floor—to reduce the impact on your knees, ankles, and lower back. Never jump rope on concrete, cement, metal, or asphalt. These surfaces are unforgiving and will increase the chance of injury.

Start with jumping intervals of 15 to 30 seconds, with rest periods of 30 to 45 seconds. Build slowly over several weeks until you can jump uninterrupted for 15 to 20 minutes or more. Be sure to stretch your calf muscles well after each session.

Drafting Runs and Cycling

Most moving objects create a draft, pulling energy toward the back of the object from behind. The field of energy behind the front object allows the objects following it to use less effort while maintaining the same velocity. Using this technique allows the person in the back to recuperate until it is his or her turn to take the lead (picture migrating geese).

If you run or cycle in a group, you can use this technique. Form a straight line and take off. The last person must overtake the leader. Continue this process of catch-the-leader until the desired time or distance is reached or until everyone has been in the lead.

For safety reasons, choose a route with little or no traffic. It may be a good idea to run or cycle on a track or in a park or forest.

Swimming

Swimming is a great cross-training exercise. It takes pressure off the back and forces the upper body to work just as hard as the lower body, unlike cycling or stair climbing. Consider taking a few lessons at your local swim center if you're unfamiliar with proper form.

Rowing Machine

Indoor rowing machines such as those used at commercial gyms provide a great full-body workout and a terrific cross-training exercise. Be sure to maintain good seated posture at all times. Use the legs as much as possible, because they have the body's biggest muscles. Exhale when pulling the handle inward.

Chapter 5

Strength, Balance, and Core Training

Because skiing and snowboarding often require bursts of speed, strength training is a powerful component in your conditioning program. As mentioned earlier, strength training consists of relatively short bursts of muscular force that last anywhere between 1 second and 2 minutes. This type of training builds size and strength in the muscles and conditions them to store more energy for immediate use.

However, after only 20 or 30 seconds of such activity, the source of immediate energy is exhausted and the muscles (and your liver) must release a form of sugar that is broken down to create even more energy. Strength training conditions the body to store more of this sugar for future needs. This chemical reaction not only allows the muscles to continue generating force but (unfortunately) also creates acid and hydrogen ions, which create a burning sensation in the muscles as they accumulate. This burning may cause you to stop your activity earlier than you intended. Strength training increases your tolerance so you can get past the burn, allowing you to carve harder and more powerfully.

Balance training enhances strength and coordination in the smaller stabilizing muscles of the body, enhances kinesthetic awareness (the mind's awareness of where the body is in space), and improves the body's sense of balance. Be sure to master executing the traditional strength training exercises with proper form and control before advancing to performing the same exercises on the balance apparatus.

Core training involves strength exercises that focus on the muscles of the trunk (the abdominals, obliques, lower back muscles, and so forth). Most exercises will incorporate flexing, extending, rotating, or side bending the spine, or a combination of movements performed in conjunction with upper and lower body motion. The purpose of core training is to strengthen the muscles that protect the back while at the same time allowing force to transfer from the center of the body down through the legs and up through the arms with the least amount of restriction.

Other benefits of strength, balance, and core training include:

- Increased energy levels.

- Reduced injury potential.

- Increased bone density.

- Increased body circulation.

- Heightened body awareness.

When performing these exercises, remember the five Rs, which are important elements of every strength program:

1. **Resistance:** The amount of weight or other resistance used during an exercise. Whatever the amount of resistance chosen, it's essential to maintain proper form while performing an exercise.

2. **Repetitions:** The number of times a movement is performed during a set of an exercise. Typically, the lower the number of repetitions (with high resistance), the more basic strength is trained; the higher the number of repetitions (with low resistance), the more muscular endurance is trained.

3. **Range of motion:** The movement a muscle is responsible for. Ideally, it is best to train the muscle's fullest range of motion.

4. **Rest:** The amount of time resting between each set of exercises. An ideal rest period is between 30 seconds and 2 minutes, but the rest period may increase with greater intensity of exercise.

5. **Recovery:** The amount of time spent between strength training workouts of the same muscle group. It is often recommended that you allow 48 hours after strength training one muscle group before exercising that same muscle group again, though this is not an iron-clad rule. If you find that you are strength training the same muscle groups two days in a row, consider changing the selection of exercises for the second day (for example, when exercising the abdominals, perform leg lifts on Monday and full sit-ups on Tuesday).

When training for strength, try to achieve temporary muscle fatigue in one set of each exercise. Temporary muscle fatigue occurs when the muscles are so exhausted that you cannot perform another repetition with proper technique.

It's important to maintain proper technique from start to finish in a set. It's equally important to have someone act as a spotter for safety when you perform exercises with weights that are suspended over your body.

Exhale during the exertion phase of each exercise (for example, as you stand upward during a squat). If you experience dizziness or pain during an exercise, stop immediately and omit that exercise from your workout for the time being.

In selecting your strength workout program, choose a range of exercises that incorporates all the major muscle groups. If you intend to perform strength workouts more than three or four times per week, it may be better to focus on the upper body on one day and the lower body on a different day.

A word about weights: Use an amount of weight that allows you to properly perform a set of no fewer than 8 repetitions and no more than 15. If you are able to perform more than 15 repetitions, increase the weight; if you cannot do 8, consider decreasing the weight. This is not to imply that performing fewer than 8 repetitions or more than 15 is wrong; it is just a general range that is safe for most people.

The exercises in this chapter provide details on how to perform them correctly, and you can refer back to these descriptions as you get into your training program. Some of the exercises also illustrate three approaches—beginning, intermediate, and advanced—to enhance program variety. Start with the beginning stage, and progress to the intermediate and advanced stages only after you can maintain proper form and body control throughout the entire exercise.

The exercises are divided into three categories: upper body, lower body, and torso (core). Each description lists the muscles involved in the exercise, and these muscles are shown in the Muscle Chart in Appendix 4.

The workout programs in Chapter 7 suggest typical schedules and provide the appropriate number of sets and repetitions for these exercises.

Some of the following exercises require a workout facility with ample equipment and space to execute the drills safely, but other exercises can be performed at home. Therefore, even if you do not belong to a gym, you can still create an effective program of strength training.

Most of the exercises have variations, which can be explained by gym staff trainers or others familiar with the routines.

Upper Body Exercises

Push-Up

1. Place your hands in a parallel position just outside shoulder width.

2. Support your body on your hands and toes. You can also start on your hand and knees, if you prefer.

3. Inhale as you lower your body until your chest barely touches the floor or until your elbows form a 90-degree angle. [1]

4. Exhale as you push back up. [2]

5. Throughout the exercise, keep your body rigid by contracting your abdominal muscles. Don't allow your back to arch or bow at any time.

Muscles involved: Pectorals, deltoids, triceps.
Benefit: Strengthens the chest, arms, and shoulder muscles.
Intermediate: Perform the same movement with your hands on a balance board. [3]

continued

upper body exercises

Push-Up, *continued*

Advanced: Perform the same movement with your hands on an Indo Board [4, 5] or with your toes on a stability ball. [6, 7]

Slide-Board Chest Fly

1. Place your hands on slippers on a slide-board (or on waxed paper plates on carpet), in a parallel position just outside shoulder width.

2. Support your body on your hands and knees. [1]

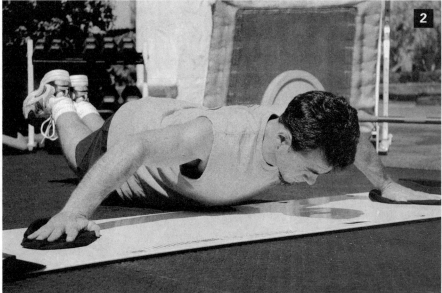

3. Inhale as you lower your body, sliding your arms out to the sides until your chest barely touches the floor. [2]

4. Exhale as you push back up.

5. Throughout the exercise, keep your body rigid by contracting your abdominal muscles. Don't allow your back to arch or bow at any time.

Muscles involved: Pectorals, deltoids, triceps.
Benefit: Strengthens the chest, arms, and shoulder muscles.

continued

Slide-Board Chest Fly, *continued*

Intermediate: Perform the same movement while supporting your body on your hands and toes. [3, 4]

Advanced: Perform the same movement with your toes supported on a balance board or stability ball. [5, 6]

Bench Dip

1. Place both hands behind you, shoulder-width apart, on the front edge of a bench, chair, or box.

2. Straighten both legs in front of you, with your feet resting on the heels and the toes pointed up. [1]

3. Straighten your arms so your body weight is supported.

4. Inhale as you bend your elbows and lower your body until your elbows and shoulders are at the same height. [2]

5. Exhale as you push your body back up to the starting position.

Muscles involved: Pectorals, deltoids, triceps.
Benefit: Strengthens the chest, shoulders, and triceps.
Intermediate: Perform the same movement with your heels resting on a box.
Advanced: Perform the same movement with your heels resting on a box and holding a weight in your lap.

Seated Row

1. Sit in a tall position, with your knees slightly bent and your feet braced on opposite sides of the cable.

2. Grip the handles in a slightly forward seated posture. [1]

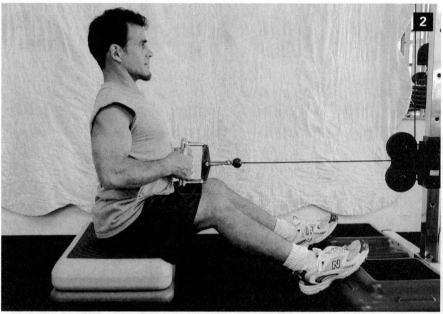

3. Exhale as you pull your arms toward your body. [2]

4. Inhale as you use your arms to return the weight to the starting position.

5. At no time during the exercise should the upper body arch back behind the hips.

Major muscles involved: Latissimus dorsi, middle trapezius, rhomboids, posterior deltoid, biceps brachii, brachioradialis.
Benefit: Strengthens the arms, shoulders, and back muscles.
Note: Grip variations include wide, narrow, and underhand.

continued

Seated Row, *continued*

Intermediate: Perform the same movement in a standard squat position. [3, 4]

upper body exercises

Advanced: Perform the same movement in a single-leg squat position.
[5, 6]

One-Arm Cable Fly

1. Sit in a tall, upright position and raise one arm directly to the side, grasping the cable handle. [1]

2 Exhale as you pull the cable in front of and across your body. [2]

3. Allow your torso to twist with the movement to involve core muscles.

4. Reach the hand that is not pulling behind your body toward the cable machine.

5. Inhale as you return to the starting position.

Muscles involved: Pectorals, abdominals, obliques.
Benefit: Strengthens the chest, shoulder, and core muscles.
Note: Variations in pulley height can be performed (high, middle, and low).

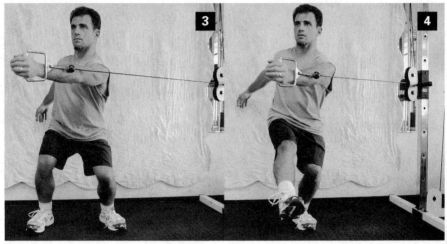

Intermediate: Perform the same movement in the standard squat position. [3]

Advanced: Perform the same movement in the single-leg squat position. [4]

One-Arm Reverse Cable Fly

1. Sit in a tall, upright position and reach the arm opposite the cable across the front of your body to grasp the cable handle. [1]

2. Exhale as you pull the cable in front of and across your body. [2]

3. Allow your torso to twist with the movement to involve core muscles.

4. Reach the hand that is not pulling behind your body toward the cable machine.

5. Inhale as you return to the starting position.

Muscles involved: Posterior deltoid, middle trapezius, obliques, rhomboids.
Benefit: Strengthens core muscles and the back of the shoulders.
Note: Variations in pulley height can be performed (high, middle, and low).

Intermediate: Perform the same movement in the standard squat position. [3]
Advanced: Perform the same movement in the single-leg squat position. [4]

upper body exercises

Dip

1. Place your hands shoulder-width apart on the dip bars.

2. Push your body up until your arms are straight and your body weight is supported. [1]

3. Inhale as you bend your elbows and lower your body until your elbows and shoulders are at the same height. [2]

4. Exhale as you push your body back up to the starting position.

Muscles involved: Deltoids, triceps, pectorals.
Benefit: Strengthens the chest, shoulders, and triceps.

Intermediate: Perform the same movement with a medicine ball clamped between your feet. [3]
Advanced: Perform the same movement with both legs straight and raised in front of you to hip height, with or without a medicine ball. [4]

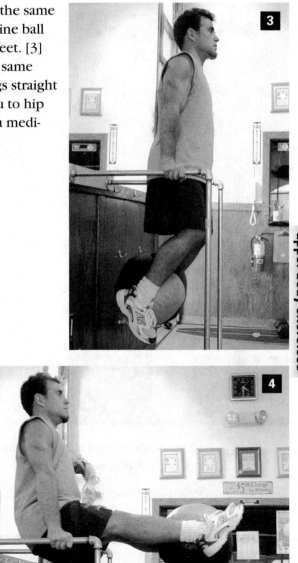

Pull-Up

1. Grasp a pull-up bar, with your hands shoulder-width apart. Start from a straight-arm hanging position. [1]

2. Exhale as you pull your body up until your chin is above the bar. [2]

3. Inhale as you lower your body back to the starting position.

4. Do not kick with your legs to help raise your body.

Muscles involved: Latissimus dorsi, middle trapezius, posterior deltoid, biceps.

Benefit: Strengthens the upper body muscles.

Intermediate: Perform the same movement with a medicine ball clamped between your feet. [3]

Advanced: Perform the same movement with a medicine ball clamped between your feet and with both legs raised straight in front of your body. [4]

Forearm Curl with Dowel

1. Stand, gripping the dowel with your arms raised straight in front of you at shoulder height.

2. Rotate your wrists back and forth to roll the suspended dumbbell up to the dowel. [1]

3. After the dumbbell has reached the top, rotate the wrists to slowly unwind the cord in the opposite direction until the dumbbell is in the starting position. [2]

Muscles involved: Forearm flexors.
Benefit: Strengthens the wrists and forearms.
Intermediate: Perform the same movement while standing on a balance board.
Advanced: Perform the same movement while standing on one leg on a balance board.

Reverse-Grip Arm Curl

1. Stand with your feet hip-width apart and your knees slightly bent.

2. Hold a barbell with a pronated (palms down) grip. [1]

3. Exhale as you bend your elbows and raise the barbell to shoulder height. [2]

4. Inhale as you lower the barbell to the starting position.

Muscles involved: Brachioradialis.
Benefit: Strengthens the wrists, forearms, and arm flexor muscles.
Intermediate: Perform the same movement while standing on a balance board. [3, 4]

continued

upper body exercises

Reverse-Grip Arm Curl, *continued*

Advanced: Perform the same movement while kneeling on a stability ball. [5, 6]

Wrist Curl

1. Stand with your feet hip-width apart and your knees slightly bent.

2. Hold a barbell with your fingers hooked in a supinated (palms up) grip. [1]

continued

upper body exercises

3. Exhale as you curl your fingers, raising the barbell until your wrists flex. [2]

4. Inhale as you uncurl your fingers until the barbell returns to the starting position.

Muscles involved: Forearm flexors.
Benefit: Strengthens the wrists and forearms.
Intermediate: Perform the same movement while standing on a balance board.
Advanced: Perform the same movement while kneeling on a stability ball.

Stick Lift

1. Stand with your feet hip-width apart and your knees slightly bent.

2. Grip a stick in one hand, pointing it toward the ground in front of you. [1]

3. Keeping your arm still, bend your wrist to raise the stick. [2]

4. Slowly lower the stick back to the starting position.

5. Repeat using the opposite hand.

Muscles involved: Forearm flexors.
Benefit: Strengthens the wrists and forearms.
Note: A baseball bat or golf club can be substituted for the stick. A snowboard works well only if you use both hands.
Intermediate: Perform the same movement while standing on a balance board.
Advanced: Perform the same movement while kneeling on a stability ball.

Lower Body Exercises

Leg Press

1. Place your feet hip-width apart and parallel. Sit with your lower back in contact with the back rest of the leg press machine. [1]

2. Inhale as you lower the weight until your knees are at right angles. [2]

3. Keep your abdominal muscles firm and your lower back pressed into the pad.

4. Exhale as you press the weight upward to the starting position.

5. Press evenly through the heels and balls of your feet at all times.

6. Do not lock your knee joints in a straight position at any time.

Muscles involved: Hamstrings, gluteals, quadriceps.
Benefit: Enhances leg and hip strength.
Intermediate: Perform the same movement but allow both feet to pivot, first to the left 45 degrees and then to the right 45 degrees. Your knees should bend in the direction your feet are pointing.
Advanced: Perform the same movement with one leg. The weight amount should be reduced by at least 50 percent.

Hack Squat

1. Place your feet hip-width apart, with your back pressing against the pad.

2. After you unlock the sled, grip the handles beside your shoulders. [1]

3. Inhale as you descend until your knees form right angles. [2]

4. Exhale as you press evenly with both legs back to the starting position.

5. Keep your abdominal muscles tightly contracted at all times.

Muscles involved:
Quadriceps, hamstrings, gluteals.

Benefit: Strengthens the hip and thigh muscles.

Intermediate: Perform the same movement but allow both feet to pivot, first to the left 45 degrees and then to the right 45 degrees. Your knees should bend in the direction your feet are pointing.

Advanced: Perform the same movement with one leg. The weight amount should be reduced by at least 50 percent.

Squat

1. Stand with your feet hip-width apart or slightly wider.

2. Rest a barbell on your shoulders, just above the shoulder blades (not on your neck). [1]

3. Inhale as you bend your knees, lowering your body until your knees are parallel with your hips. Your back should be in a slightly arched position at all times. [2]

4. Exhale as you return your body to the starting position.

5. Weight should be placed on the heels.

6. Keep your head position neutral or slightly upward.

Muscles involved: Gluteals, hamstrings, quadriceps.

Benefit: Strengthens the legs and torso while focusing on balance.

Intermediate: Perform the same movement while standing on a balance board. [3, 4]

continued

Squat, *continued*

Advanced: Perform the same movement while standing on an Indo Board. [5, 6] Or perform the same movement while keeping the barbell over your head throughout. Keep your arms straight at all times. [7, 8]

Split Squat

1. Rest a barbell on your shoulders, just above the shoulder blades (not on the neck).

2. Step forward with your right foot, placing it about 3 feet ahead of your left foot. [1]

3. Inhale as you bend both legs at the knees and hips.

4. Lower your body until your right (forward) knee and right hip are parallel (your left knee should be about an inch from the floor). [2]

5. Exhale and reverse direction until your legs are almost straight.

6. Repeat with your left leg forward.

7. Do not let the forward knee bend past your toes; keep your shin and knee perpendicular to the ground.

Muscles involved: Gluteals, hamstrings, quadriceps.
Benefit: Strengthens the legs in two positions while focusing on balance.

Intermediate: Perform the same movement with your front foot on a balance board. [3, 4]

continued

Split Squat, *continued*

Advanced: Hold a medicine ball with both hands. With your front foot on a balance board, twist your torso in the direction of your forward leg. [5, 6]

Squat with Torso Rotation

1. Stand with your feet hip-width apart and your knees slightly bent while holding a medicine ball in both hands. [1]

2. Inhale while lowering your body until your knees are parallel with your hips and rotating your upper body to the right. [2]

3. Keep your back slightly arched at all times.

4. Exhale as you return your body to the starting position.

continued

Squat with Torso Rotation, *continued*

5. On the next repetition, rotate your upper body to the left. [3]

6. Weight should be placed on the heels.

7. Keep your head position neutral or slightly upward.

Muscles involved: Gluteals, quadriceps, hamstrings, obliques. **Benefit:** Strengthens the legs and torso while focusing on balance.

Intermediate: Perform the same movement while standing on a balance board. [4, 5]

continued

Squat with Torso Rotation, *continued*

Advanced: Perform the same movement while standing on an Indo Board. [6, 7]

lower body exercises

Single-Leg Squat

1. Stand on your left leg with your arms and right leg extended in front of your body. [1]

2. Inhale as you bend your left leg at the knees and hips.

3. Descend as low as possible, keeping your left heel on the ground and your right heel as close to the ground as possible. [2]

4. Exhale as you push up to the starting position.

5. Repeat using the right leg.

Muscles involved: Quadriceps, hamstrings, gluteals.
Benefit: Strengthens the legs while focusing on single-leg balance.

continued

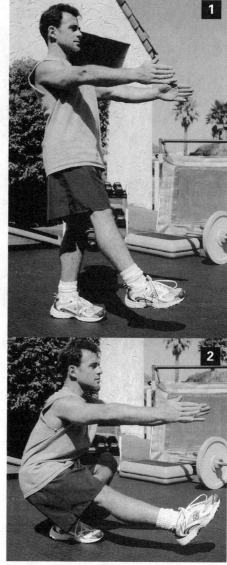

lower body exercises

Single-Leg Squat, *continued*

Intermediate: Perform the same movement while standing on a balance board. [3]

Advanced: Perform the same movement while standing on a balance board with your eyes closed or blindfolded. [4]

Side Squat with Slide-Board

1. Stand at the end of a
   slide-board with your
   left foot on a slipper
   (or on a waxed paper
   plate on carpet) and
   with your right foot on
   the floor. [1]

   continued

Side Squat with Slide-Board, *continued*

2. Inhale as you lower your body and slide your left leg out to the side until your right knee is parallel with your hips. [2]

3. Exhale as you return your body to the starting position.

4. Keep your back slightly arched at all times and make sure the majority of your body weight is supported by your right leg.

5. Keep your head position neutral or slightly upward.

6. Perform 10 to 15 repetitions.

7. Repeat using the opposite leg.

Muscles involved: Gluteals, hamstrings, quadriceps, leg adductors.
Benefit: Strengthens the legs and torso while focusing on balance.
Intermediate: Perform the same movement with your standing leg on a balance board.

Advanced: Perform the same movement with your standing leg on a balance board while you rotate your torso toward the standing leg's side while holding a medicine ball.

Wall Sit

1. Sit against a wall or door so your lower back is flat and your knees and hips are the same height from the floor—as if you were sitting on a chair. [1]

2. Your feet should be 5 inches apart, pointing straight ahead and parallel.

3. Your feet should be away from the wall so the heels are directly below your knees and your toes are raised slightly off the floor.

4. Your ankles, knees, and hips should all be at right angles.

5. The weight of your body should be pressed through your heels and not the toes.

6. Hold for 30 seconds to 2 minutes.

Muscles involved: Rectus femoris.
Benefit: Enhances leg strength and proper posture and reduces lower back tension.

lower body exercises

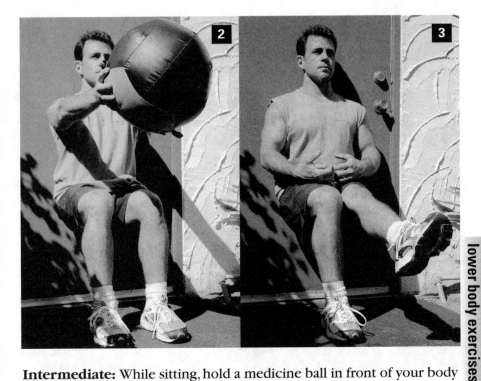

Intermediate: While sitting, hold a medicine ball in front of your body with outstretched arms. [2]

Advanced: While sitting, lift one leg off the floor and hold for the desired time. Repeat, lifting the opposite leg. [3]

Step Up

1. Place your right foot flat on a box 12 to 18 inches high. [1]

2. Exhale as you step up on the box, bringing your bent left knee up to hip height and flexing your left foot up. [2]

3. Inhale as you return the left foot to the floor.

4. Perform 8 to 15 repetitions.

5. Repeat using the opposite leg.

Muscles involved: Quadriceps, hamstrings, gluteals.

Benefit: Strengthens the hips and thighs while enhancing single-leg balance.

Intermediate: Perform the same movement, but on the return do not let the foot touch the floor (keep it just an inch away from touching) so the leg that is on the box supports your weight through the entire set.

Advanced: Perform the same movement but on the return bring your foot down in front of the box instead of behind it. Alternate touching the floor in front and behind the box with each repetition. [3]

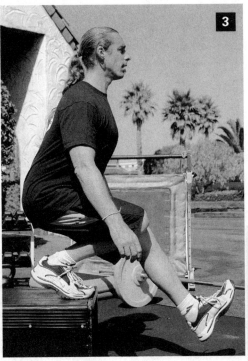

Front Lunge

1. Stand upright, feet hip-width apart and parallel, while holding a dumbbell in each hand or placing your hands by your hips. [1]

2. Inhale as you take a step forward with your right foot. [2]

3. Descend until your right knee is directly above your right heel (your hips and forward knee should be at the same height). [3]

4. Exhale as you push off the floor with your right leg and return to the starting position.

5. Keep the upper body upright at all times. Be sure the hips and shoulders move forward at the same time, and do not allow your shoulders to push back first.

6. Perform 8 to 15 repetitions.

7. Repeat using the opposite leg.

Muscles involved: Quadriceps, hamstrings, gluteals.
Benefit: Strengthens the legs in forward motion while focusing on balance and change of direction.

continued

Front Lunge, *continued*

lower body exercises

Intermediate: Perform the same movement with a dumbbell in each hand, but while stepping forward and descending, reach forward with the dumbbells so that, at the bottom of the movement, your chest is resting against your forward thigh and the dumbbells are in front of your forward foot. [4]

Advanced: Perform the same movement with a dumbbell in each hand, but while stepping forward and descending, rotate the head and torso to the side of the forward leg. [5]

Reverse Lunge

1. Stand upright, feet hip-width apart and parallel, while holding a dumbbell in each hand or placing your hands by your hips. [1]

2. Inhale as you take a step backward with your left foot.

3. Descend until your right knee is directly above your right heel (your hips and forward knee should be at the same height). [2]

4. Exhale as you push off the floor with your left leg and use your right leg to pull your body back up to the starting position.

5. Keep your upper body upright at all times; do not allow your shoulders to push forward first.

6. Perform 8 to 15 repetitions.

7. Repeat, stepping backward with your right foot.

Muscles involved: Gluteals, hamstrings, quadriceps.

Benefit: Strengthens the legs in backward motion while focusing on balance and change of direction.

continued

lower body exercises

Reverse Lunge, *continued*

Intermediate: Perform the same movement with a dumbbell in each hand, but while stepping backward and descending, reach forward with the dumbbells so that at the bottom of the movement your chest is resting against your forward thigh and the dumbbells are in front of your forward foot. [3]

Advanced: Perform the same movement with a dumbbell in each hand, but while stepping backward and descending, rotate the head and torso to the side of the forward leg. [4]

Lateral Lunge

1. Stand with your right foot pointing forward and your left foot pointing outward (to the left). [1]

2. Inhale as you take a step to the left with your left foot.

3. Descend until your left knee is directly above the left heel. [2]

4. Exhale as use your left leg to push your body back to the starting position.

5. Keep your upper body upright at all times; do not allow your shoulders to push forward first.

6. Perform 8 to 15 repetitions.

7. Repeat, stepping with the right leg.

Muscles involved: Gluteals, hamstrings, quadriceps, leg adductors.
Benefit: Strengthens the legs in lateral motion while focusing on balance and change of direction.

continued

Lateral Lunge, *continued*

Intermediate: Perform the same movement with a dumbbell in each hand, but while stepping to the side, reach forward with the dumbbells so that, at the bottom of the movement, your chest is resting against the thigh of your stepping leg and the dumbbells are in front of your foot. [3]

lower body exercises

Advanced: Perform the same movement with a dumbbell in each hand, but while stepping to the side, laterally rotate your head and torso to the side of your stepping leg. [4]

Curtsy Lunge

1. Stand with your feet together, holding a dumbbell in each hand. [1]
2. Inhale as you take a step with your right foot behind and to the left of your left leg.
3. Descend until your left knee is above your left heel but not past the toes. [2]
4. Exhale as you use both legs to pull your body back to the starting position.
5. Keep your shoulders above your hips at all times, making sure they move laterally at the same time.
6. Perform 8 to 15 repetitions.
7. Repeat, stepping with your left foot.

Muscles involved: Quadriceps, hamstrings, gluteals, leg abductors.
Benefit: Strengthens the legs in lateral motion while focusing on balance and change of direction.
Intermediate: Perform the same movement with a dumbbell in each hand, but while stepping, reach forward with the dumbbells so that, at the bottom of the movement, your chest is resting against your forward thigh and the dumbbells are in front of your foot. [3]
Advanced: Perform the same movement with a dumbbell in each hand, but while stepping, laterally rotate your head and torso to the side of your stepping leg. [4]

lower body exercises

Inner Thigh Pull

1. Attach the ankle strap to your left leg, with the ring on the outside of the leg.

2. Stand on your right foot with your left leg extended to the side. [1]

3. Maintaining a tall, upright posture, exhale as you pull your left leg in front of your right leg. [2]

4. Inhale as you return to the starting position.

5. Keep your abdominal muscles tight to protect your lower back.

6. Repeat using the opposite leg.

Muscles involved: Leg adductors.
Benefit: Strengthens the hip and inner thigh muscles.

Outer Thigh Pull

1. Attach the ankle strap to your right leg, with the ring on the inside of the leg.

2. Stand on your left foot, with the ankle strap clipped to the low pulley so the cable crosses in front of your left leg. [1]

3. Maintaining a tall, upright posture, exhale as you pull your right leg to the right. Move only as far as a straight posture will allow. [2]

4. Inhale as you return to the starting position.

5. Keep your abdominal muscles tight to protect your lower back.

6. Repeat using the opposite leg.

Muscles involved: Leg abductors.
Benefit: Strengthens the outer hip and thigh muscles while promoting single-leg balance.

Calf Raise

1. Stand on a step with both heels hanging off the edge. If you like, you can use a pole for balance. [1]

2. Exhale as you raise your body to a tiptoe position. [2]

3. Inhale as you lower your heels as far as possible.

Muscles involved: Gastrocnemius, soleus.
Benefit: Strengthens the calf muscles.

Toe Raise

1. Stand on a step with your toes and the balls of your feet touching the floor. Use a pole for balance if you like.

2. Exhale as you lift your toes as high as possible. [2]

3. Inhale as you lower your toes to the floor.

Muscles involved: Anterior tibialis.
Benefit: Strengthens the muscles in the front of the lower leg.

Toe Pull

1. Attach an ankle strap around the ball of your right foot, with the ring on the sole side of the foot.

2. Connect the low pulley cable to the strap on your right foot. [1]

3. Maintaining a tall, seated posture, pull the toes of your right foot toward you and hold the position for 3 seconds. [2]

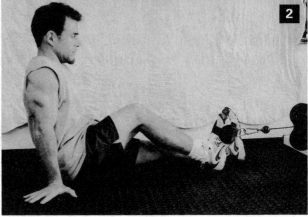

4. Slowly return your foot to the starting position.

5. Perform 10 to 15 repetitions.

6. Repeat using the opposite foot.

Muscles involved: Anterior tibialis.
Benefit: Enhances knee stability.

Ankle Alphabet

1. Lie on your back with your right leg raised above your hip and with your right knee bent at a right angle.

2. Keep your leg still as you trace the letters of the alphabet with your right foot.

3. Repeat using the opposite leg.

Muscles involved: Anterior tibialis.

Benefit: Promotes proper ankle movement and knee stability.

Foot Circles and Point Flexes

1. Lie on your back with your right leg raised above your hip and with your knee bent at a right angle.

2. Keep your leg still as you make circles in a clockwise direction with your right foot. [1]

3. Make circles in a counterclockwise direction.

4. Point your foot and then flex it back toward you. [2]

5. Repeat the exercise using the opposite foot.

Muscles involved:
Anterior tibialis.

Benefit: Promotes proper ankle movement and knee stability.

Torso (Core) Exercises

Leg Lift with Abdominal Straps

1. Place your arms through the straps so the straps rest against your armpits.

2. Grip one strap in each hand and lift your feet off the ground so you are hanging in the straps. [1]

3. Exhale as you lift your knees to your elbows. [2]

4. Inhale as you return to the hanging position.

Muscles involved: Psoas major, latissimus dorsi, rectus abdominis, quadriceps.

Benefit: Strengthens the torso and hip flexor muscles.

continued

torso (core) exercises

Leg Lift with Abdominal Straps, *continued*

Intermediate: Perform the same movement with a medicine ball clamped between your feet. [3]

Advanced: Perform the same movement with your legs extended straight in front of you and with a medicine ball clamped between your feet. [4]

Twisting Leg Lift with Abdominal Straps

1. Place your arms through the straps so the straps rest against your armpits.

2. Grip one strap in each hand and lift your feet off the ground so you are hanging in the straps.

3. Exhale as you lift your left knee to your right elbow.

4. Inhale as you return to the hanging position.

5. Repeat lifting your right knee to your left elbow.

Muscles involved: Psoas major, latissiums dorsi, rectus abdominis, lateral and external obliques, quadriceps.

Benefit: Strengthens the torso and hip flexor muscles.

Intermediate: Perform the same movement but lift both knees lifting to one elbow and then to the other.

Advanced: Perform the same movement with a medicine ball clamped between your feet while lifting both knees to one elbow and then to the other.

torso (core) exercises

Overhead Medicine Ball Toss

1. Lie on your back with your knees bent at right angles and your feet flat on the floor.

2. With both hands over your head, grip a medicine ball. [1]

3. Exhale as you curl your body upward and hurl the ball forward with your arms. [2]

4. Inhale as the ball returns and you lower your body back to the starting position.

5. You will need either a partner to catch and return the ball or trampoline-like equipment angled to bounce the ball back to you.

Muscles involved: Psoas major, rectus abdominis, latissimus dorsi.
Benefit: Strengthens the abdominals and trunk flexion.

Crunch on Stability Ball

1. Lie on a stability ball so your middle and lower back are resting on the ball and your feet are on the floor, hip-width apart. Clasp your hands behind your head. [1]

2. With your clasped hands supporting your head, exhale and lift your middle back off the ball. [2]

3. Inhale as you return to the starting position.

Muscles involved: Rectus abdominis.
Benefit: Strengthens the abdominal muscles.

continued

torso (core) exercises

Crunch on Stability Ball, *continued*

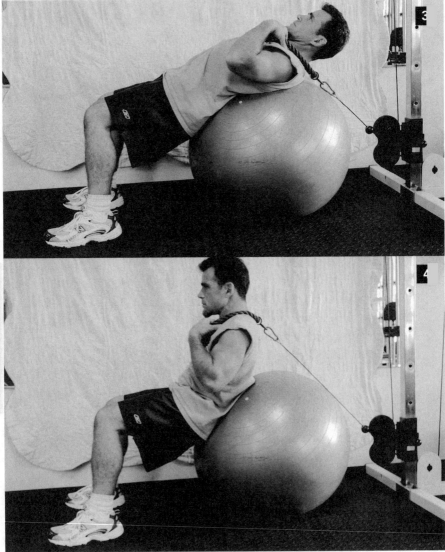

Intermediate: Perform the same movement while holding a rope handle attached to a low pulley with weights. [3, 4]

torso (core) exercises

Advanced: Perform the same movement while holding a rope handle attached to a low pulley with weights and with one leg raised off the floor. [5]

Side Bend on Stability Ball

1. Lie on your left side on a stability ball, with your legs in a split position and feet on the floor. Clasp your hands behind your head or cross your arms over your chest. [1]

2. Exhale as you bend sideways, lifting your upper body off the ball. [2]

3. Inhale as you return to the starting position.

Muscles involved: Internal and external obliques.

Benefit: Strengthens the oblique muscles.

torso (core) exercises

Intermediate: Perform the same movement with your arms extended over your head. [3]
Advanced: Perform the same movement with your arms extended over your head while holding a medicine ball. [4]

Lying Torso Rotation on Stability Ball

1. Lie on a stability ball so your shoulders and middle back are resting on the ball and your feet are on the floor, hip-width apart. Clasp your hands together and extend your arms above your chest. [1]

2. Inhale as you rotate your upper body to the right until your arms are parallel to the floor. [2]

3. Exhale as you return to the starting position.

4. Repeat rotating to the left.

Muscles involved: Gluteals, hamstrings, quadriceps, abdominals, spinal erectors, and internal and external obliques.

Benefit: Strengthens the abdominals and the oblique muscles.

torso (core) exercises

Intermediate: Perform the same movement while holding a dumbbell with both hands. [3, 4]

Advanced: Perform the same movement while holding a dumbbell in each hand; never let the dumbbells touch each other. [5]

Back Extension on Stability Ball

torso (core) exercises

1. Lie on your stomach on a stability ball so your lower chest and mid-section rest on the ball and your toes are hip-width apart on the floor. Clasp your hands behind your neck. [1]

2. Exhale as you lift your chest and midsection off the ball until your body forms a straight line. [2]

3. Inhale as you return to the starting position.

Muscles involved: Spinal erectors, gluteals, hamstrings, middle trapezius, rhomboids.

Benefit: Strengthens the lower back muscles.

Intermediate: Perform the same movement with your arms extended in front of you. [3]

continued

torso (core) exercises

Back Extension on Stability Ball, *continued*

Advanced: Perform the same movement with your arms extended in front of you and holding a medicine ball. [4]

Baseball Swing

1. Stand perpendicular to the left-side pulley, with both hands gripping a rope handle and the legs hip-width apart with the knees slightly bent. [1]

2. Keeping your arms straight, exhale as you pull your arms across your body to your right, similar to swinging a baseball bat. [2]

3. Inhale as you return to the starting position but do not let the weight stack rest.

4. Perform a set facing the opposite direction, and rotate to your left.

Muscles involved: Internal and external obliques.
Benefit: Strengthens the upper body and torso muscles.
Note: Variations in pulley position (high, middle, and low) can change the concentration placed on your muscles. Maintain the same basic form regardless of pulley height.
Intermediate: Perform the same movement while standing on a balance board.
Advanced: Perform the same movement while standing on one leg on a balance board.

torso (core) exercises

Ax Chop

1. Begin in a bent-over position with your legs 3 feet apart and your arms between your legs and holding a medicine ball. [1]

2. Keeping your arms rigid but slightly bent at the elbows, inhale as you lift the ball over your head. [2]

3. Exhale as you return to the starting position.

Muscles involved: Spinal erectors, abdominals, gluteals, psoas major.

Benefit: Strengthens the arms, shoulders, and torso muscles.

torso (core) exercises

Intermediate: Perform the same movement while standing on a balance board. [3]

Advanced: Perform the same movement while standing on an Indo Board. [4]

Torso Rotation in Square Stance

1. Stand with your legs 3 feet apart and your knees slightly bent.

2. Hold a medicine ball with both hands in front of your body at chest height.

3. Keep your arms rigid but slightly bent at the elbows.

4. Rotate your arms and torso to the left. [1]

5. Rotate your arms and torso to the right. [2]

Muscles involved: Gluteals, quadriceps, hamstrings, internal and external obliques.
Benefit: Strengthens the arms, shoulders, and torso muscles.

Intermediate: Perform the same movement while standing on a balance board. [3]

Advanced: Perform the same movement while standing on an Indo Board. [4]

torso (core) exercises

Lateral Torso Raise

1. Lie on your left side with both legs together and your left elbow propped under your left shoulder. [1]

2. Exhale as you lift your hips off the floor until just your left foot remains on the floor; the leg should not touch the ground. [2]

3. Inhale as you lower your body back to the starting position.

4. Repeat, lying on your right side.

Muscles involved: Hip abductors, obliques, latissimus dorsi.
Benefit: Strengthens your shoulder joints and the sides of your torso.

Intermediate: Perform the same movement while supporting your upper body with your hand and straight arm instead of your elbow. [3]

continued

torso (core) exercises

Lateral Torso Raise, *continued*

Advanced: Perform the same movement while supporting your upper body with your hand and straight arm instead of your elbow. While your hips are off the ground, lift the upper leg. [4] Or perform the same movement while supporting your upper body with your hand and straight arm instead of your elbow and while resting your feet on a balance board.

Chapter 6

Plyometric Training

Snowboarding and skiing require quick reflexes, powerful turns, and explosive reactions. Just lifting a bunch of dumbbells and stretching is not going to train the body to respond in that manner. This is where plyometric training comes in. Olympic athletes have been using plyometric exercises for decades to become record-breaking high jumpers, triple jumpers, and skiers. Now that snowboarding is an Olympic event, plyometrics are being introduced to aerial and half-pipe competitors.

Plyometrics should *not* be performed on concrete, cement, or any other surface that does not absorb impact. The repetitive, ballistic nature of these exercises is very demanding on the body, so choose a forgiving surface—such as one that is wooden or padded or a sandy or grassy area—to reduce the risk of injury.

Single-Leg Hop

1. Stand on your left leg, with your elbows bent at right angles and your hands slightly clenched. [1]

2. Crouch slightly, then hop on your left foot while swinging your arms upward. [2, 3]

3. The swinging action of your arms should occur only at your shoulders, allowing your hands to travel from your hips toward your chin and back to your hips.

Benefit: Increases single-leg power and balance.

Double-Leg Hop

1. Stand on both legs, with your feet parallel and hip-width apart. Keep your elbows bent at right angles and your hands slightly clenched.

2. Crouch slightly, then hop repeatedly while swinging your arms upward. [1, 2]

3. The swinging action of your arms should occur only at your shoulders, allowing your hands to travel from your hips toward your chin and back to your hips.

Benefit: Increases lower leg reflexes, balance, and power.

Lateral Jump

1. Stand on your right leg. Keep your elbows bent at right angles and your hands slightly clenched. [1]

2. Crouch slightly, then jump sideways and land on your left foot while swinging your arms to the left. [2]

3. The swinging action of your arms should occur only at your shoulders, allowing your elbows to travel side to side.

plyometric training

4. Reverse directions by jumping off your left foot and swinging your elbows to the right. [3]

Benefit: Focuses on lateral stability, reflexes, and power.

Front and Back Jumps

1. Stand on both legs. Keep your elbows bent at right angles and your hands slightly clenched.

2. Crouch slightly, then jump forward 3 to 5 feet while swinging your arms forward. [1, 2]

3. The swinging action of your arms should occur only at your shoulders, allowing your hands to travel from your hips toward your chin and back to your hips.

4. Facing the same direction, rebound backward to the starting point.

Benefit: Increases hip and leg explosiveness and trains the body to change directions quickly.

Twisting Jump

1. Stand on both legs. Keep your elbows bent at right angles and your hands slightly clenched.

2. Crouch slightly, then jump backward and rotate your body to your left 180 degrees, swinging your arms to the left, so you land facing the opposite direction. [1, 2]

3. The swinging action of your arms should occur only at the shoulders.

4. Reverse directions by jumping backward and 180 degrees to the right and swinging the elbows to the right. [3]

Benefit: Focuses on quick reflexes and direction changes while maintaining balance.

Box or Stair Jump

1. Stand on both legs. Keep your elbows bent at right angles and your hands slightly clenched.

2. Crouch slightly, then jump up on a box or a step and step back down to the floor. [1, 2]

3. The swinging action of your arms should occur only at your shoulders.

Benefit: Increases vertical jump while reducing impact on the body.
Note: The higher the box or step, the more intense the exercise level.

Single-Leg Box or Stair Jump

1. Stand on both legs. Keep your elbows bent at right angles and your hands slightly clenched.

2. Crouch slightly, then jump up on a box or a step with your left leg and step back down to the floor. [1, 2]

3. The swinging action of your arms should occur only at the shoulders.

4. Repeat using the opposite leg.

Benefit: Focuses on single-leg vertical jump while reducing impact on the body.

Note: The higher the box or step, the more intense the exercise level.

plyometric training

Multiple Box or Stair Jump

1. Stand on both legs. Keep your elbows bent at right angles and your hands slightly clenched.

2. Crouch slightly, then jump repeatedly up on a box or a step and gently jump back down to the floor. [1, 2]

3. The swinging action of your arms should occur only at the shoulders.

4. Try to spend more time in the air than you do on the ground.

Benefit: Trains power (explosiveness) and quick reaction to ground forces.

Note: The higher the box or step, the more intense the exercise level.

Twisting Box Jump

1. Stand on both legs. Keep your elbows bent at right angles and your hands slightly clenched.

2. Crouch slightly, then jump up sideways, swinging your arms to your right while rotating your body to the right 90 degrees and landing on the top of the box briefly. [1, 2, 3]

continued

plyometric training

Twisting Box Jump, *continued*

3. Jump gently off the box, continuing to turn to your right another 90 degrees so you land on the ground facing the opposite direction from the starting point. [4, 5]

4. The swinging action of your arms should occur only at the shoulders.

5. Reverse directions by jumping to your left.

Benefit: Trains the body to change directions while reacting to ground forces and maintaining balance.

plyometric training

Tuck Jump

1. Stand on both legs, with your arms raised straight over your head. [1]

2. Jump off the ground and bring your knees up toward your chest.

3. With both hands, grab your legs just below the knees. [2]

4. Land on both feet with your arms back in the starting position.

Benefit: Increases hip power in both directions (flexion and extension).

plyometric training

Twisting Tuck Jump

1. Stand on both legs, with your arms raised straight over your head. [1]

2. Jump off the ground and bring your knees up toward your chest as you rotate your body to the right. [2]

3. With both hands, grab your legs just below the knees. [3]

4. Land on both feet with your arms back over your head and your body facing in the opposite direction from the starting position. [4, 5]

5. Repeat, turning to your left.

Benefit: Increases hip power in both directions (flexion and extension) while change in direction challenges balance and coordination.

plyometric training

Chapter 7

Sample Workout Programs

Now that all of the components of a snowriding conditioning program have been discussed in detail, it is time to put your own program together. The sample workouts provided here can help. Each workout has three parts: flexibility, endurance, and strength. Although the flexibility portion appears first, remember that most gains occur when stretching is performed at the end of a workout. Each flexibility routine includes lying, kneeling, sitting, and standing stretches. Be sure to select a few from each group with each program you design. The Sun Salutation is not included with the samples. Instead, use the Sun Salutation as a wake-up or warm-up routine as often as possible. It will increase your flexibility and energize you first thing in the morning.

Each endurance program blends indoor and outdoor exercises. Depending on weather conditions, you may be forced to use more indoor endurance exercises—but, if possible, create a blend. Labels of "low," "moderate," and "high" are given to describe the intensity level of an exercise. "Low" refers to 60 to 70 percent of maximum heart rate and 5 to 6 on the scale of the rate of perceived exertion (RPE). "Moderate" is 70 to 80 percent of maximum heart rate and 6 to 7 on the RPE scale. "High" refers to 80 to 90 percent of maximum heart rate and 7 to 9 on the RPE scale.

The strength programs combine upper body, lower body, and torso exercises as well as plyometric exercises. Several exercises incorporate stability balls, medicine balls, and balance boards. If you have access to this type of equipment, incorporate them into your routine as often as possible. If not, create as much variety in the other exercises as possible. Emphasize the exercises that are challenging. Too often people focus on the exercises that are their "strong suits," performing these exercises more than any others, which creates strength imbalances (one muscle stronger than its counterpart). Imbalances lead to improper movement, and improper movements increase the chance of injury. Part of this approach is to *find* the exercises that are challenging. The true challenge is not to bench-press 300 pounds; rather, it is to find the weaker muscles and improve their strength.

Not all exercises appearing in this book are included in the sample routines. I didn't want you to simply copy my routines. Be original! Be creative! Use the variety and information provided here to create your own program. Refer as often as you like to the photos and descriptions of the various exercises. The flexibility exercises are in Chapter 2; endurance exercises, in Chapter 4; strength exercises, in Chapter 5; and plyometric exercises, in Chapter 6. See Appendix 1 for a list of all exercises, and refer to the index to locate the page number for a specific exercise by name.

Home Program

Gyms and health clubs aren't your cup of tea? Too many muscleheads? Too much fluorescent spandex? Whatever the issue, don't worry—you don't have to join the sweatshops. The following sample routines can be performed in the comfort and privacy of your home. Do consider investing in a few dumbbells, a medicine ball, a stability ball, and perhaps a balance board. These accessories will increase the number of exercises available to you.

Home Program: Weeks 1 and 2

Flexibility Training Exercises: Monday, Tuesday, Thursday, Friday

Exercise	Sets	Time
Crossed Knee Lift	2	30 sec. per side
Crossover Twist	2	30 sec. per side
Kneeling Groin Stretch	2	30 sec. per leg
Child's Pose	1	1 min.
Archer Pose	1	1 min.
Wrist Stretch 1	2	30 sec. per wrist
Squat Pose 1	2	30 sec.
Standing Forward Bend	2	30 sec.

Aerobic Conditioning: Saturday, Tuesday, Thursday

Fill in your heart rate, if you want to keep a record of it.

Exercise	Duration	Heart Rate	RPE
Walking	20 min.		4 to 6
Stair Climbing	20 min.		7 to 8

Strength Training Exercises: Monday, Wednesday, Friday

Write in the amount of weight you're using to keep track of your progress.

Exercise	Set 1 Weight/Reps.	Set 2 Weight/Reps.
Push-Up	body weight/15	body weight/15
Bench Dip	body weight/15	body weight/15
Step Up	___ lbs./15	___ lbs./15
Front Lunge	___ lbs./15	___ lbs./15
Calf Raise	body weight/15	body weight/15
Crunch on Stability Ball	body weight/15	body weight/15
Side Bend on Stability Ball	body weight/15	body weight/15
Single-Leg Hop	body weight/10	body weight/10
Lateral Jump	body weight/10	body weight/10

Home Routine: Weeks 3 and 4

Flexibility Training Exercises: Monday, Tuesday, Thursday, Friday

Exercise	Sets	Time
Upper Spinal Floor Twist	2	30 sec. per side
Calf Stretch with Strap	2	30 sec. per leg
Reclining Hero Pose	2	30 sec.
Mad Cat Stretch	1	1 min.
Sitting Floor	1	1 min.
Simple Twist	2	30 sec. per side
Reverse Triangle Pose	2	30 sec. per side
Doorknob Stretch	2	30 sec.

Aerobic Conditioning Exercises: Saturday, Tuesday, Thursday

Fill in your heart rate, if you want to keep a record of it.

Exercise	Duration	Heart Rate	RPE
Skateboarding	1 hour		4 to 6
Jumping Rope	10 min.		7 to 8
Surfing	60 min.		5 to 7

Strength Training Exercises: Monday, Wednesday, Friday

Write in the amount of the weight you're using to keep track of your progress.

Exercise	Set 1 Weight/Reps.	Set 2 Weight/Reps.	Set 3 Weight/Reps.
Dip	body weight/15	body weight/15	body weight/15
Squat	__ lbs./15	__ lbs./15	__ lbs./15
Wall Sit	body weight/1 min.	body weight/1 min.	body weight/1 min.
Lateral Lunge	__ lbs./15	__ lbs./15	__ lbs./15
Ankle Alphabet	body weight/15	body weight/15	body weight/15
Back Extension on Stability Ball	body weight/15	body weight/15	body weight/15
Ax Chop	__ lbs./15	__ lbs./15	__ lbs./15
Lateral Torso Raise	body weight/20	body weight/20	body weight/20
Double-Leg Hop	body weight/10	body weight/10	body weight/10
Twisting Jump	body weight/10	body weight/10	body weight/10
Tuck Jump	body weight/10	body weight/10	body weight/10

Home Routine: Weeks 5 and 6

Flexibility Training Exercises: Monday, Tuesday, Thursday, Friday

Exercise	Sets	Time
Straight-Leg Hamstring Stretch with Strap	2	30 sec. per leg
Bridge Pose	2	30 sec.
Arm Circles	2	1 min.
Shoulder Pivots	2	1 min.
Archer Pose	2	30 sec.
Wrist Twist	3	15 sec. per wrist
Squat Pose 1	2	30 sec.
Dancer's Pose	2	30 sec. per leg
Arm Stretch	2	30 sec.

Aerobic Conditioning Exercises: Saturday, Tuesday, Thursday

Fill in your heart rate, if you want to keep a record of it.

Exercise	Duration	Heart Rate	RPE
Stair Climbing	20 min.		5 to 7
Jumping Rope	20 min.		7 to 8
Trampoline Work	45 min.		5 to 7

Strength Training Exercises: Monday, Wednesday, Friday

Write in the amount of weight you're using to keep track of your progress.

Exercise	Set 1 Weight/Reps.	Set 2 Weight/Reps.	Set 3 Weight/Reps.
Pull-Up	body weight/15	body weight/15	body weight/15
Forearm Curl with Dowel	__ lbs./15	__ lbs./15	__ lbs./15
Squat with Torso Rotation	__ lbs./15	__ lbs./15	__ lbs./15
Single-Leg Squat	__ lbs./15	__ lbs./15	__ lbs./15
Lateral Lunge and Curtsy Lunge	__ lbs./15	__ lbs./15	__ lbs./15
Toe Raise	__ lbs./15	__ lbs./15	__ lbs./15
Overhead Medicine Ball Toss	__ lbs./25	__ lbs./25	__ lbs./25
Side Bend on Stability Ball	body weight/25	body weight/25	body weight/25
Front and Back Jumps	body weight/10	body weight/10	body weight/10
Twisting Jump	body weight/10	body weight/10	body weight/10
Twisting Tuck Jump	body weight/10	body weight/10	body weight/10

Home Routine: Weeks 7 and 8

Flexibility Training Exercises: Monday, Tuesday, Thursday, Friday

Exercise	Sets	Time
Straight-Leg Hamstring Stretch with Strap	2	30 sec. per leg
Intense Front Stretch	2	30 sec.
Kneeling Groin Stretch	2	30 sec. per leg
Child's Pose	1	1 min.
Downward Dog	2	1 min.
Fingers and Toes Entwined	2	30 sec. per leg
Wrist Stretch 2	3	15 sec. per wrist
Warrior Pose	2	30 sec. per side
Standing Forward Bend	2	30 sec.

Aerobic Conditioning Exercises: Saturday, Tuesday, Thursday

Fill in your heart rate, if you want to keep a record of it.

Exercise	Duration	Heart Rate	RPE
Running	30 min.		4 to 6
Drafting Runs	30 min.		7 to 8
Rowing Machine	20 min.		6 to 7

Strength Training Exercises: Monday, Wednesday, Friday

Write in the amount of weight you're using to keep track of your progress.

Exercise	Set 1 Weight/Reps.	Set 2 Weight/Reps.	Set 3 Weight/Reps.
Push-Up (on Balance Board)	body weight/15	body weight/15	body weight/15
Dip	__ lbs./15	__ lbs./15	__ lbs./15
Split Squat	__ lbs./15	__ lbs./15	__ lbs./15
Side Squat with Slide-Board	__ lbs./15	__ lbs./15	__ lbs./15
Step Up	__ lbs./15	__ lbs./15	__ lbs./15
Back Extension on Stability Ball	body weight/15	body weight/15	body weight/15
Torso Rotation in Square Stance	__ lbs./15	__ lbs./15	__ lbs./15
Lateral Torso Raise	body weight/15	body weight/15	body weight/15
Front and Back Jumps	body weight/10	body weight/10	body weight/10
Box or Stair Jump	body weight/10	body weight/10	body weight/10
Twisting Box Jump	body weight/10	body weight/10	body weight/10

Home Routine: Weeks 9 and 10

Flexibility Training Exercises: Monday, Tuesday, Thursday, Friday

Exercise	Sets	Time
Bow Pose	2	30 sec.
Upward Dog	2	30 sec.
Hero Pose	2	30 sec.
Mad Cat Stretch	1	1 min.
Downward Dog	2	1 min.
Seated Torso Twist	2	30 sec. per side
Wrist Stretch 2	3	15 sec. per wrist
Side Reach	2	30 sec. per side
Squat Pose 2	2	30 sec.
Arm Stretch	2	30 sec.

Aerobic Conditioning Exercises: Saturday, Tuesday, Thursday

Fill in your heart rate, if you want to keep a record of it.

Exercise	Duration	Heart Rate	RPE
Swimming	30 min.		4 to 6
Drafting Runs	45 min.		8 to 10
Slide-Board	20 min.		6 to 7

Strength Training Exercises: Monday, Wednesday, Friday

Write in the amount of weight you're using to keep track of your progress.

Exercise	Set 1 Weight/Reps.	Set 2 Weight/Reps.	Set 3 Weight/Reps.
Slide-Board Chest Fly	body weight/15	body weight/15	body weight/15
Reverse-Grip Arm Curl	__ lbs./15	__ lbs./15	__ lbs./15
Stick Lift	stick/15	stick/15	stick/15
Reverse Lunge	__ lbs./15	__ lbs./15	__ lbs./15
Curtsy Lunge	__ lbs./15	__ lbs./15	__ lbs./15
Calf Raise	body weight/25	body weight/25	body weight/25
Toe Raise	body weight/25	body weight/25	body weight/25
Leg Lift with Abdominal Straps	body weight/25	body weight/25	body weight/25
Twisting Leg Lift with Abdominal Straps	body weight/25	body weight/25	body weight/25
Single-Leg Box or Stair Jump	body weight/10	body weight/10	body weight/10
Twisting Box Jump	body weight/10	body weight/10	body weight/10
Twisting Tuck Jump	body weight/10	body weight/10	body weight/10

Gym Program

Are you a member of a gym or thinking of joining one in the near future? The following routines are samples of what your gym routine might look like. Some machines may differ from the ones featured in this book. If you are unfamiliar with the equipment, be certain to ask a staff member for help.

One more thing: remember gym etiquette. Please carry a workout towel to wipe your perspiration off machines, and be sure to allow other members to share equipment you are using when you are between sets. Your fellow gym members will thank you.

Gym Routine: Weeks 1 and 2

Flexibility Training Exercises: Monday, Tuesday, Thursday, Friday

Exercise	Sets	Time
Crossed Knee Lift	2	30 sec. per side
Crossover Twist	2	30 sec. per side
Kneeling Groin Stretch	2	30 sec. per leg
Child's Pose	1	1 min.
Archer Pose	1	1 min. per side
Wrist Stretch 1	2	30 sec. per wrist
Squat Pose 1	2	30 sec.
Standing Forward Bend	2	30 sec.

Aerobic Conditioning Exercises: Saturday, Tuesday, Thursday

Fill in your heart rate, if you want to keep a record of it.

Exercise	Duration	Heart Rate	RPE
Walking	20 min.		4 to 6
Stair Climbing	20 min.		7 to 8

Strength Training Exercises: Monday, Wednesday, Friday

Write in the amount of weight you're using to keep track of your progress.

Exercise	Set 1 Weight/Reps.	Set 2 Weight/Reps.
Push-Up	body weight/15	body weight/15
Seated Row	__ lbs./15	__ lbs./15
Leg Press	__ lbs./15	__ lbs./15
Step Up	__ lbs./15	__ lbs./15
Front Lunge	body weight/15	body weight/15
Leg Lift with Abdominal Straps	body weight/15	body weight/15
Side Bend on Stability Ball	body weight/15	body weight/15
Single-Leg Hop	body weight/10	body weight/10
Lateral Jump	body weight/10	body weight/10

Gym Routine: Weeks 3 and 4

Flexibility Training Exercises: Monday, Tuesday, Thursday, Friday

Exercise	Sets	Time
Upper Spinal Floor Twist	2	30 sec. per side
Calf Stretch with Strap	2	30 sec. per leg
Reclining Hero Pose	2	30 sec.
Mad Cat Stretch	1	1 min.
Sitting Floor	1	1 min. per side
Simple Twist	2	30 sec. per side
Reverse Triangle Pose	2	30 sec. per side
Doorknob Stretch	2	30 sec.

Aerobic Conditioning Exercises: Saturday, Tuesday, Thursday

Fill in your heart rate, if you want to keep a record of it.

Exercise	Duration	Heart Rate	RPE
Skateboarding	1 hour		4 to 6
Jumping Rope	10 min.		7 to 8
Swimming	20 min.		6 to 7

Strength Training Exercises: Monday, Wednesday, Friday

Write in the amount of weight you're using to keep track of your progress.

Exercise	Set 1 Weight/Reps.	Set 2 Weight/Reps.	Set 3 Weight/Reps.
Dip	body weight/15	body weight/15	body weight/15
Squat	__ lbs./15	__ lbs./15	__ lbs./15
Lateral Lunge	__ lbs./15	__ lbs./15	__ lbs./15
Outer Thigh Pull	__ lbs./15	__ lbs./15	__ lbs./15
Ankle Alphabet	body weight/15	body weight/15	body weight/15
Back Extension on Stability Ball	body weight/15	body weight/15	body weight/15
Baseball Swing	__ lbs./15	__ lbs./15	__ lbs./15
Ax Chop	__ lbs./15	__ lbs./15	__ lbs./15
Double-Leg Hop	body weight/10	body weight/10	body weight/10
Twisting Jump	body weight/10	body weight/10	body weight/10
Tuck Jump	body weight/10	body weight/10	body weight/10

Gym Routine: Weeks 5 and 6

Flexibility Training Exercises: Monday, Tuesday, Thursday, Friday

Exercise	Sets	Time
Straight-Leg Hamstring Stretch with Strap	2	30 sec. per leg
Bridge Pose	2	30 sec.
Arm Circles	2	1 min.
Shoulder Pivots	2	1 min.
Archer Pose	2	30 sec. per side
Wrist Twist	3	15 sec. per wrist
Squat Pose 1	2	30 sec.
Dancer's Pose	2	30 sec. per side
Arm Stretch	2	30 sec.

Aerobic Conditioning Exercises: Saturday, Tuesday, Thursday

Fill in your heart rate, if you want to keep a record of it.

Exercise	Duration	Heart Rate	RPE
Stair Climbing	20 min.		5 to 7
Jumping Rope	20 min.		7 to 8
Trampoline Work	45 min.		5 to 7

Strength Training Exercises: Monday, Wednesday, Friday

Write in the amount of weight you're using to keep track of your progress.

Exercise	Set 1 Weight/Reps.	Set 2 Weight/Reps.	Set 3 Weight/Reps.
Pull-Up	body weight/15	body weight/15	body weight/15
Forearm Curl with Dowel	__ lbs./15	__ lbs./15	__ lbs./15
Squat with Torso Rotation	__ lbs./15	__ lbs./15	__ lbs./15
Single-Leg Squat	__ lbs./15	__ lbs./15	__ lbs./15
Wall Sit	body weight/1 min.	body weight/1 min.	body weight/1 min.
Inner Thigh Pull	__ lbs./15	__ lbs./15	__ lbs./15
Overhead Medicine Ball Toss	__ lbs./25	__ lbs./25	__ lbs./25
Side Bend on Stability Ball	body weight/25	body weight/25	body weight/25
Front and Back Jumps	body weight/10	body weight/10	body weight/10
Twisting Jump	body weight/10	body weight/10	body weight/10
Twisting Tuck Jump	body weight/10	body weight/10	body weight/10

Gym Routine: Weeks 7 and 8

Flexibility Training Exercises: Monday, Tuesday, Thursday, Friday

Exercise	Sets	Time
Straight-Leg Hamstring Stretch with Strap	2	30 sec. per leg
Intense Front Stretch	2	30 sec.
Kneeling Groin Stretch	2	30 sec. per leg
Child's Pose	1	1 min.
Downward Dog	2	1 min.
Fingers and Toes Entwined	2	30 sec. per leg
Wrist Stretch 2	3	15 sec. per wrist
Warrior Pose	2	30 sec. per side
Standing Forward Bend	2	30 sec.

Aerobic Conditioning Exercises: Saturday, Tuesday, Thursday

Fill in your heart rate, if you want to keep a record of it.

Exercise	Duration	Heart Rate	RPE
Running	30 min.		4 to 6
Drafting Runs	30 min.		7 to 8
Rowing Machine	20 min.		6 to 7

Strength Training Exercises: Monday, Wednesday, Friday

Write in the amount of weight you're using to keep track of your progress.

Exercise	Set 1 Weight/Reps.	Set 2 Weight/Reps.	Set 3 Weight/Reps.
One-Arm Cable Fly	___ lbs./15	___ lbs./15	___ lbs./15
One-Arm Reverse Cable Fly	___ lbs./15	___ lbs./15	___ lbs./15
Split Squat	___ lbs./15	___ lbs./15	___ lbs./15
Side Squat with Slide-Board	___ lbs./15	___ lbs./15	___ lbs./15
Step Up	___ lbs./15	___ lbs./15	___ lbs./15
Twisting Leg Lift with Abdominal Straps	body weight/15	body weight/15	body weight/15
Torso Rotation in Square Stance	___ lbs./15	___ lbs./15	___ lbs./15
Lateral Torso Raise	body weight/15	body weight/15	body weight/15
Front and Back Jumps	body weight/10	body weight/10	body weight/10
Box or Stair Jump	body weight/10	body weight/10	body weight/10
Twisting Box Jump	body weight/10	body weight/10	body weight/10

Gym Routine: Weeks 9 and 10

Flexibility Training Exercises: Monday, Tuesday, Thursday, Friday

Exercise	Sets	Time
Bow Pose	2	30 sec.
Upward Dog	2	30 sec.
Hero Pose	2	30 sec.
Mad Cat Stretch	1	1 min.
Downward Dog	2	1 min.
Seated Torso Twist	2	30 sec. per side
Wrist Stretch 2	3	15 sec. per wrist
Side Reach	2	30 sec. per side
Squat Pose 2	2	30 sec.
Arm Stretch	2	30 sec.

Aerobic Conditioning Exercises: Saturday, Tuesday, Thursday

Fill in your heart rate, if you want to keep a record of it.

Exercise	Duration	Heart Rate	RPE
Swimming	30 min.		4 to 6
Drafting Runs	45 min.		8 to 10
Slide-Board	20 min.		6 to 7

Strength Training Exercises: Monday, Wednesday, Friday

Write in the amount of weight you're using to keep track of your progress.

Exercise	Set 1 Weight/Reps.	Set 2 Weight/Reps.	Set 3 Weight/Reps.
Seated Row	__ lbs./15	__ lbs./15	__ lbs./15
Reverse-Grip Arm Curl	__ lbs./15	__ lbs./15	__ lbs./15
Stick Lift	stick/15	stick/15	stick/15
Hack Squat	__ lbs./15	__ lbs./15	__ lbs./15
Reverse Lunge	__ lbs./15	__ lbs./15	__ lbs./15
Curtsy Lunge	__ lbs./15	__ lbs./15	__ lbs./15
Toe Raise	body weight/25	body weight/25	body weight/25
Leg Lift with Abdominal Straps	body weight/25	body weight/25	body weight/25
Twisting Leg Lift with Abdominal Straps	body weight/25	body weight/25	body weight/25
Single-Leg Box or Stair Jump	body weight/10	body weight/10	body weight/10
Twisting Box Jump	body weight/10	body weight/10	body weight/10
Twisting Tuck Jump	body weight/10	body weight/10	body weight/10

Appendix 1

Following is a list of all exercises described in this book, categorized by whether they are aimed mainly at promoting flexibility, endurance, or strength. You can use this list to personalize your workouts, selecting from a variety of these exercises to adapt the workout programs in Chapter 7 to suit your particular conditioning goals.

Check the chapters indicated in order to review the photos and descriptions of any of these exercises.

Flexibility Exercises
(Chapter 2)

Lying Stretches (choose 2 to 4)

Crossed Knee Lift
Crossover Twist
Upper Spinal Floor Twist
Straight-Leg Hamstring Stretch
    with Strap
Calf Stretch with Strap
Intense Front Stretch
Locust Pose
Bridge Pose
Bow Pose
Upward Dog

Kneeling Stretches (choose 2 to 4)

Hero Pose
Reclining Hero Pose
Kneeling Groin Stretch
Kneeling Single Quadriceps
    Stretch
Child's Pose
Mad Cat Stretch
Downward Dog
Arm Circles
Shoulder Pivots

Sitting Stretches (choose 2 to 4)

Fingers and Toes Entwined
Archer Pose
Sitting Floor
Simple Twist
Seated Torso Twist
Wrist Stretch 1
Wrist Stretch 2
Wrist Twist

Standing Stretches (choose 2 to 4)

Triangle Pose
Reverse Triangle Pose
Warrior Pose
Side Reach
Extended Toe-to-Hand Pose
Squat Pose 1

Squat Pose 2
Doorknob Stretch
Dancer's Pose
Standing Forward Bend
Arm Stretch
Wrist Stretch

Sun Salutation
(Chapter 3)

Prayer Pose
Mountain Pose
Forward Bend
Lunge Position
Plank Position
Grasshopper Pose
Upward-Facing Dog
Downward-Facing Dog
Lunge Position
Deep Forward Bend
Mountain Pose
Prayer Pose

Endurance Exercises
(Chapter 4)

(choose 1 to 3 for each workout session)

Skateboarding
Surfing
Slide-Board
Trampoline Work
Walking and Running
Stair Climbing

Jumping Rope
Drafting Runs and Cycling
Swimming
Rowing Machine

Strength Exercises
(Chapter 5)

Upper Body Exercises (choose 1 to 3)

Push-Up
Slide-Board Chest Fly
Bench Dip
Seated Row
One-Arm Cable Fly
One-Arm Reverse Cable Fly
Dip
Pull-Up
Forearm Curl with Dowel
Reverse-Grip Arm Curl
Wrist Curl
Stick Lift

Lower Body Exercises (choose 3 to 5)

Leg Press
Hack Squat
Squat
Split Squat
Squat with Torso Rotation
Single-Leg Squat
Side Squat with Slide-Board
Wall Sit
Step Up

Lower Body Exercises, *continued*

Front Lunge
Reverse Lunge
Lateral Lunge
Curtsy Lunge
Inner Thigh Pull
Outer Thigh Pull
Calf Raise
Toe Raise
Toe Pull
Ankle Alphabet
Foot Circles and Point Flexes

Torso (Core) Exercises (choose 3 to 5)

Leg Lift with Abdominal Straps
Twisting Leg Lift with Abdominal Straps
Overhead Medicine Ball Toss
Crunch on Stability Ball
Side Bend on Stability Ball

Lying Torso Rotation on Stability Ball
Back Extension on Stability Ball
Baseball Swing
Ax Chop
Torso Rotation in Square Stance
Lateral Torso Raise

Plyometric Exercises
(Chapter 6)

(choose 2 to 4)

Single-Leg Hop
Double-Leg Hop
Lateral Jump
Front and Back Jumps
Twisting Jump
Box or Stair Jump
Single-Leg Box or Stair Jump
Multiple Box or Stair Jump
Twisting Box Jump
Tuck Jump
Twisting Tuck Jump

Appendix 2

Workout Log

Devotion **2** Motion CONSULTANTS

Workout #1

Cardiovascular Conditioning

Type of Exercise	Ht. Rate	Duration	R.P.E.

Strength Training

Name of Exercise	Set 1	Set 2	Set 3
1			
2			
3			
4			
5			
6			
7			
8			
9			
10			

Flexibility Training

1			
2			
3			
4			
5			
6			
7			
8			

Workout #2

Type of Exercise	Ht. Rate	Duration	R.P.E.

Name of Exercise	Set 1	Set 2	Set 3
1			
2			
3			
4			
5			
6			
7			
8			
9			
10			

1			
2			
3			
4			
5			
6			
7			
8			

Workout #3

Type of Exercise	Ht. Rate	Duration	R.P.E.

Name of Exercise	Set 1	Set 2	Set 3
1			
2			
3			
4			
5			
6			
7			
8			
9			
10			

1			
2			
3			
4			
5			
6			
7			
8			

www.DEVOTION2MOTION.net

Devotion 2 Motion Consultants®

Workout #1

Cardiovascular Conditioning

Type of Exercise	Ht. Rate	Duration	R.P.E.
Running	160	30min.	7 to 8
Skateboarding	110	1 hr	5 to 6

Strength Training

Name of Exercise	Set 1	Set 2	Set 3
1. Push Up	bw/15	bw/15	bw/12
2. Dips	bw/15	bw/12	bw/9
3. Squat	20/15	20/15	30/13
4. Adv. Lateral Lunge	15/15	15/15	15/15
5. Side Bend on Ball	bw/30	bw/25	bw/20
6. Baseball Swing	20/15	25/15	30/12
7. Ax Chop	15/15	15/15	20/14
8. Single Leg Hop	bw/8	bw/8	bw/8
9. Dbl Leg Hop	bw/8	bw/8	bw/8
10. Tuck Jump	bw/5	bw/5	bw/5

Flexibility Training

Name of Exercise		
1. Upper Sp. Flr. Twist	30 sec.	30 sec.
2. Calf Stretch w/ Strap	30 sec.	30 sec.
3. Reclining Hero's Pose	30 sec.	30 sec.
4. Mad Cat Stretch	30 sec.	30 sec.
5. Sitting Floor	30 sec.	30 sec.
6. Simple Twist	30 sec.	30 sec.
7. Rev. Triangle Pose	30 sec.	30 sec.
8. Doorknob Stretch	30 sec.	30 sec.

www.DEVOTION2MOTION.net

Workout #2

Type of Exercise	Ht. Rate	Duration	R.P.E.
Jumping Rope	165	20min.	8 to 9
Running	150	40min.	6 to 7

Name of Exercise	Set 1	Set 2	Set 3
1. Pull Up	bw/12	bw/10	bw/8
2. F.arm Curl w/ Dowel	15/15	15/15	15/15
3. Sq. w/ Torso Rot.	15/15	15/15	15/15
4. Single Leg Squat	bw/12	bw/10	bw/8
5. Wall Sit	1 min	1 min	1 min
6. Ovrhd. Med. Ball Toss	20/30	20/25	20/25
7. Side Bend on Ball	bw/30	bw/25	bw/20
8. Front & Back Jump	bw/8	bw/8	bw/8
9. Twisting Jump	bw/8	bw/8	bw/8
10. Twisting Tuck Jump	bw/5	bw/5	bw/5

Name of Exercise		
1. Hams. Str. w/ Strap	30 sec.	30 sec.
2. Bridge Pose	30 sec.	30 sec.
3. Arm Circles	30 sec.	30 sec.
4. Shoulder Pivots	30 sec.	30 sec.
5. Archer Pose	30 sec.	30 sec.
6. Wrist Twist	30 sec.	30 sec.
7. Squat Pose I	30 sec.	30 sec.
8. Arm Stretch	30 sec.	30 sec.

Workout #3

Type of Exercise	Ht. Rate	Duration	R.P.E.
Walking	110	30min.	4 to 5
Cycling	140	1 hr.	6 to 8
Trampoline Work	120	30min.	5 to 6

Name of Exercise	Set 1	Set 2	Set 3
1. 1-Arm Cable Fly	20/15	20/15	30/13
2. 1-Arm Rev. Cable Fly	15/15	15/15	15/15
3. Split Squat	15/15	15/15	20/14
4. Side Sq. w/ Slide Bd.	15/15	15/15	30/13
5. Step Up	20/15	20/15	30/13
6. Tw. Leg Lift w/ Strap	bw/30	bw/30	bw/20
7. Tor. Rot. In Sq. Stan.	15/15	15/15	15/15
8. Lat. Torso Raise	bw/8	bw/30	bw/25
9. Box Jump	bw/8	bw/8	bw/20
10. Twisting Box Jump	bw/5	bw/5	bw/5

Name of Exercise		
1. Str. Leg Ham Str.	30 sec.	30 sec.
2. Intense Frnt. Stretch	30 sec.	30 sec.
3. Kneeling Groin Str.	30 sec.	30 sec.
4. Child's Pose	30 sec.	30 sec.
5. Downward Dog	30 sec.	30 sec.
6. Fingers & Toes Entw.	30 sec.	30 sec.
7. Wrist Stretch II	30 sec.	30 sec.
8. Warrior Pose	30 sec.	30 sec.

Appendix 3

Resources

Alter, Michael J. *Sport Stretch.* 2nd ed. Champaign, IL: Human Kinetics, 1998.

Baechle, Thomas R., and Roger Earle, eds. *Essentials of Strength Training and Conditioning.* 2nd ed. Champaign, IL: Human Kinetics, 2000.

Couch, Jean. *The Runner's Yoga Book: A Balanced Approach to Fitness.* Berkeley, CA: Rodmell, 1990.

Muscle Balance and Function Development, www.musclebalance function.com.

Appendix 4

Muscle Chart

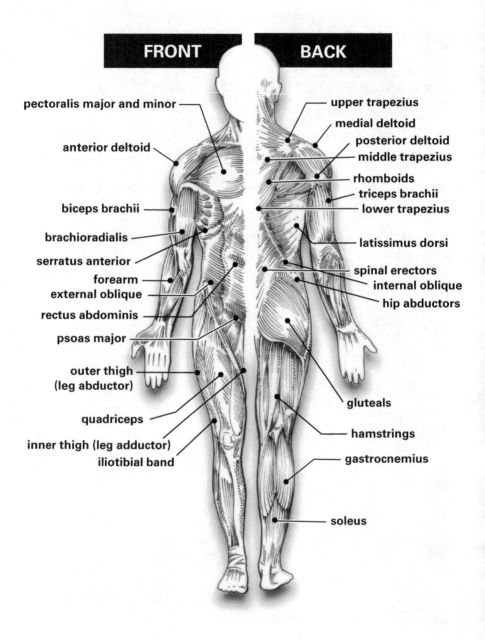

FRONT

BACK

pectoralis major and minor

anterior deltoid

biceps brachii

brachioradialis

serratus anterior

forearm

external oblique

rectus abdominis

psoas major

outer thigh
(leg abductor)

quadriceps

inner thigh (leg adductor)

iliotibial band

upper trapezius

medial deltoid

posterior deltoid

middle trapezius

rhomboids

triceps brachii

lower trapezius

latissimus dorsi

spinal erectors

internal oblique

hip abductors

gluteals

hamstrings

gastrocnemius

soleus

Index